ENERGY FOLLOWS THOUGHT

ALSO BY WILLIE NELSON

Willie Nelson's Letters to America

Me and Sister Bobbie: True Tales of the Family Band

It's a Long Story: My Life

Roll Me Up and Smoke Me When I Die: Musings from the Road

Pretty Paper: A Novel

Me and Paul: Untold Stories of a Fabled Friendship

ENERGY FOLLOWS THOUGHT
The Stories Behind My Songs

WILLIE NELSON with David Ritz and Mickey Raphael

WILLIAM MORROW
An Imprint of HarperCollinsPublishers

· CONTENTS ·

(4)

ONLY TRUE LOVE LINGERS ON

...OSE WILL DIE AND FADE AWAY
SOON ITS FRAGRANCE IS GONE
SUNSHINE ENDS AT THE CLOSE OF DAY
ONLY TRUE LOVE LINGERS ON

...E YOU NOTICED THE BIRDS ARE BEGINNING
SING
COME FALL THEIR CHURPING IS GONE
REMEMBER ONE THING WHEN YOUR
DING BELLS RING
TRUE LOVE LINGERS ON.

THE END
BY WILLIE NELSON

XV

Starting Tonight
By Willie Nelson

Starting Tonight
Your Daddy gonna start living right
Starting Tonight
I'll never more roam.
Starting tonight
Your Daddy gonna change a mite,
Your Daddy gonna stay at home,
Starting Tonight
Your Daddy gonna sweet down
Starting Tonight
I'll always be true
Starting tonight
I'm gonna quit my running round
Your Daddy coming home to you.
Chorus
I went away and left you,
oh so long ago
But now I'm coming back to you
you know I miss you so.

Starting tonight
I'll quit this silly game I've played
Starting tonight
I mean it you'll see
Starting tonight, there's gonna be a
change made, there gonna be a
big change, Starting tonight

T

THE MOON WAS YOUR HELPER

THE MOON WAS YOUR HELPER TO XXXXX HELP
XXXX YOU STEAL MY HEART
SHINNING WITH ITS SPLENDOR ABOVE
THE MOON WAS YOUR HELPER AND IT HAS DONE
ITS PART
FOR I AM SO IN LOVE.

BUT THE MOON WAS NOT NEEDED
YOU WOULD HAVE SUCCEEDED
IN STEALING MY HEART YOU KNEW

BUT THE MOON WAS YOUR HELPER TO HELP
YOU STEAL MY HEART
AND I LOVE THE MOON AND YOU.

THE END
BY WILLIE NELSON

SWEETHEARTS FOREVER

DEAR LETS BE SWEETHEARTS FOREVER
THRU WIND AND RAIN ILL BE THE SAME T...
YOU KNOW ILL NERE LEAVE YOU NEVER
THO SKIES ARE GRAY
ANOTHER DAY
WILL COME AND WHEN THOSE
CLOUDS ROLL AWAY
AND YOUR MINE FOR ALWAYS
ILL STILL BELONG
TO YOU ALONE SWEETHEART.

THE END
BY WILLI...

---

(3)

ILL WONDER ALONE

ILL WONDER ALONE
WITH A HEART THATS XXXXX TORN,
ALWAYS REMEMBERING THE LOVE WE HAVE KNOWN,
AND WITH YOU ON MY MIND THE WHOLE DAY LONG
ILL WEEP DEAR AND WONDER ALONE.

NO ONE TO CARE FOR ME WHEN THINGS GO WRONG,
NO ONE TO CRY FOR ME WHEN I AM GONE,
...TH YOU ON MY MIND THE WHOLE DAY LONG
...D DEAR AND WONDER ALONE

THE END
BY WILLIE NELSON

L

THE END
BY WIL...

AND I WONDER
REMEMBER IF YOU EVER DREAM OF ME TOO
HEART JUST THE...
COMES BACK TO ME
MEMORIES SAY...
GONE
AND ITS REWARDS...
THERE FILLED OF LOVE
MY HEARTS FILLED STILL LINGER PAIN
MANY MEMORIES SO LONG AGO
MANY DAYS HAVE COME AND GONE
LONG AGO

---

(6)

FADED LOVE AND WASTED DREAMS

ITS COLD THE NIGHTS ARE LONG AND IM SO LONELY
THE HOURS PASS ALONG LIKE YEARS IT SEEMS
ILL HEAR YOU SAY NO MORE O XXXXX LOVE YOU
ONLY
AND I THINK OF FADED LOVE AND WASTED DREAMS.

TWAS NOT SO LONG AGO I WAS SO HAPPY
YOU SAID MY DARLING PLEASE HAVE FAITH IN ME
I SHOULD XXXXXX HAVE KNOWN YOUD BREAK
MY HEART AND LEAVE ME
WITH ONLY FADED LOVE AND WASTED DREAMS.

I KNOW ILL NERE XXX FORGET THAT DAY WE PARTED
I KNEW OUR LOVE WAS JUST A MEMORY
YOUR EYES SHOWED YOU WERE GLAD THAT IT WAS
OVER
BUT MINE SHOWED ONLY PAIN AND MISERY.

WHILE WRITTING YOU THIS LAST AND FINAL LETTER
I THINK OF LOVE THAT ONCE SO BRIGHTLY BEAM...
AND IF XXXXXXXX BY CHANCE Y...
MY NAME DEAD

---

(9)

HANGOVER BLUES

WELL I WAKE UP IN THE MORNING AND I M FEELING
MIGHTY SAD
NOT A NICKLE IN MY POCKET BUT A JUG BESIDE
MY BED
I GOT THE HANGOVER BLUES
....
AND THEY HAVE SHO HAVE GOT ME DOW...

WELL I M WONDERING WHAT I M DOING
I DONE THE NIGHT BEFORE
...AD A LITTLE TOO MUCH WHISKEY AND I
WANT NO MORE
I GOT THE HANGOVER BLUES
....
AND THEY SHO DO GET ME DOWN.

I WAS WALKING HOME FROM WORK AND THOU...
I D HAVE A LITTLE DRINK
WELL I WOKE THREE HOURS LATER WITH S...
MORE DRUNKS IN THE CLINK
I GOT THE HANGOVER BLUES
....
AND THEY SHO HAVE GOT ME DOWN.

...OU CAN KEEP YO ROTGUT WHISKEY YOU CAN KE...
YO GIN AND RYE
I LL QUIT WAKING UP WITH HEADACHES AND A
WISHING I COULD DIE
DON T WANT NO HANGOVER BLUES
....
YODEL
YOU CAN KEEP YO HANGOVER BLUES.

THE END
BY WILLIE NELSON

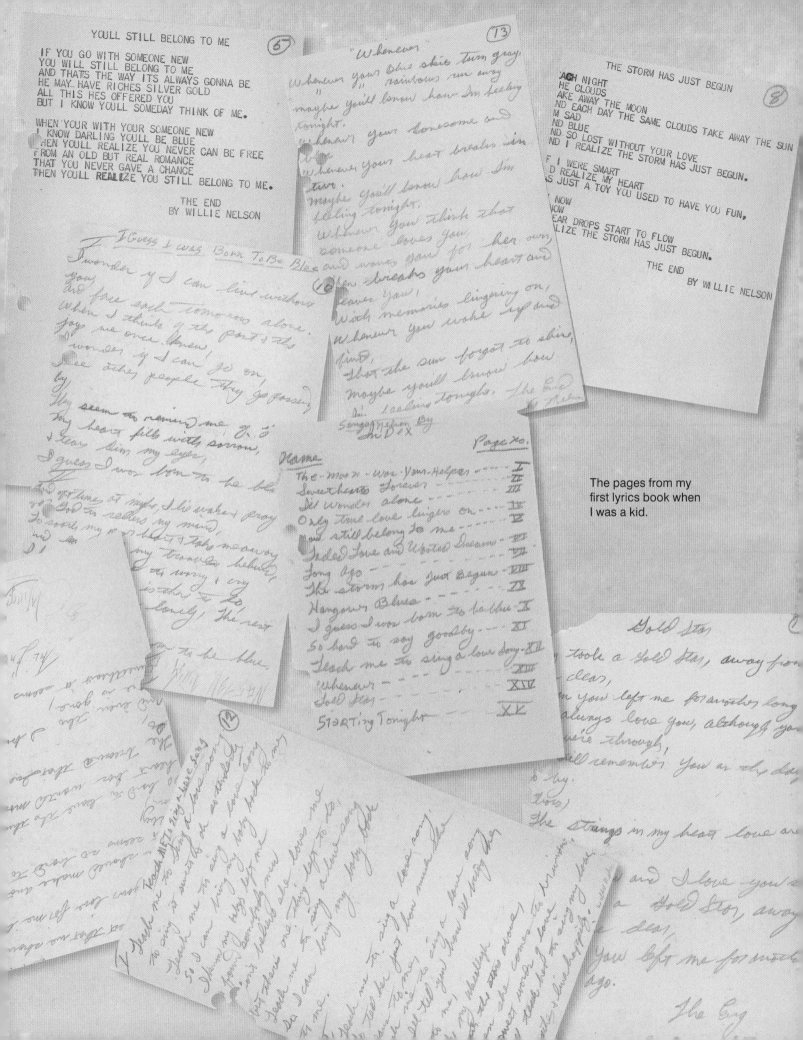

YOULL STILL BELONG TO ME

IF YOU GO WITH SOMEONE NEW
YOU WILL STILL BELONG TO ME
AND THATS THE WAY ITS ALWAYS GONNA BE
HE MAY HAVE RICHES SILVER GOLD
ALL THIS HES OFFERED YOU
BUT I KNOW YOULL SOMEDAY THINK OF ME.

WHEN YOUR WITH YOUR SOMEONE NEW
I KNOW DARLING YOULL BE BLUE
THEN YOULL REALIZE YOU NEVER CAN BE FREE
FROM AN OLD BUT REAL ROMANCE
THAT YOU NEVER GAVE A CHANCE
THEN YOULL REALIZE YOU STILL BELONG TO ME.

THE END
BY WILLIE NELSON

THE STORM HAS JUST BEGUN

EACH NIGHT
THE CLOUDS
TAKE AWAY THE MOON
AND EACH DAY THE SAME CLOUDS TAKE AWAY THE SUN
IM SAD
AND BLUE
AND SO LOST WITHOUT YOUR LOVE
AND I REALIZE THE STORM HAS JUST BEGUN.

IF I WERE SMART
ID REALIZE MY HEART
WAS JUST A TOY YOU USED TO HAVE YOU FUN,
NOW
I KNOW
TEAR DROPS START TO FLOW
REALIZE THE STORM HAS JUST BEGUN.

THE END
BY WILLIE NELSON

The pages from my
first lyrics book when
I was a kid.

· INTRODUCTION ·

When it comes to songs, I'm a patient man.
I don't try to push or prod them. I just let them happen, just
like this book is happening. I never thought about separating
my words from my music. They go together like ham and eggs.
Although unlike ham and eggs, I don't cook them at the same
time.

The words always come first. I figure that once I get the words
right, melodies will appear. They always have. Get the story
down first and it'll sing on its own.

The energy driving my words remains a mystery to me.
Those words have been popping into my head ever since I was
a little kid putting together my first little book of songs. I never
questioned that mystery or tried to figure it out. Figure it out and
it's no longer a mystery. And the thing about mysteries is that
they're fun. I don't want to take the fun out of my songs—even
those that aren't funny.

I want to keep the mystery. By doing that, you're naturally free
to interpret them however you like. Whatever they mean to you is
fine with me. You probably understand them better than I do.

I love talking about these songs and recollecting what was
running through my mind when I wrote them. But as far as
pinning down exactly what they mean . . . well, let me quote
myself on that very subject . . .

TO MAKE A LONG STORY SHORT

I see nothing to be gained by explanations
No need to try to say who's right or who was
    wrong
No need to enter into lengthy dissertations
To make a long story short she's gone

I won't attempt to explain the things that
    happened
To put in words why she's not here would
    take too long
It's all too far beyond the realm of
    understanding
To make a long story short she's gone

The way you look at me you don't believe she
    loved me
But she once loved me with a love so sweet
    and strong
And I won't try to give the reasons why I
    miss her so
To make a long story short she's gone

In the studio with Fred Carter Jr. and producer Fred Foster.

That song was written back in the early sixties. I got help from my good friend Fred Foster, one of the few producers who understood me when I was trying to make it in Nashville.

I like the feeling of "To Make a Long Story Short" because that's my mantra when it comes to lyrics. Less is more. You'll see how some aren't any more than eight lines. In most of my songs, I tend to repeat the choruses two or three times. Here on the page, I've kept them stripped down so they read right. I love short songs. Say what you got to say in three minutes or less.

Good storytelling is disciplined storytelling. The discipline comes in editing yourself. Understand that your listener doesn't have all day to hear you moan and groan. Moaning and groaning are important; it's important to get your feelings out so they don't tear you up inside. But get to the heart of those feelings—and keep it to a minimum. In doing so, you'll have the maximum effect.

It might not look like I followed my own principle in a book that's jammed with 160 songs. But keep in mind, I've written over a thousand. And every day I'm writing new ones. So yes, I've done some whittling.

Because I'm not an orderly man, I've kept the order of this collection loose. I'm not adhering to a strict timeline of when a song was written or where or why. Instead, I've grouped the lyrics according to mood.

You'll hear me chattering in between songs, and I'll say only what comes to my heart. I see these lyrics as little postcards from a long life. I see them as expressions of sadness or joy, fear or frustration, heartache and hope that are all part of our daily struggle to stay sane.

Without those songs, I might have gone insane. They let me vent whatever needed venting.

Sometimes they correspond to real events in my life. Other times I'm just making up stories that I tried to write in a way that's relatable to average folks like me.

Songwriting isn't exactly average work, but it's hardly the only work I've done. I've worked dozens of different jobs, including pumping gas and raising hogs. But the one I love best is writing and making music. I'd rather write a lyric than plow a field. I'd rather write a song than paint a barn. I loved picking cotton when I was a kid, but the moment I found a way to make money making music, I was gone.

Now that we're talking about money, here's the first group of songs, most of them written in Houston in the late fifties when I was in my twenties. I was down and out. Didn't have a clue of what a song might be worth. All I knew is that I had to write them.

FIFTY BUCKS a SONG

It took me a while to realize that songs can mean big money.
As a naive kid, I figured that just like the songs sung by birds belong to everyone, so do songs sung by humans. Didn't know the first thing about copyrights and publishing. Maybe because songs came to me so easily, I never considered them work. Consequently, I didn't understand their monetary worth. I barely had enough money to buy food and pay the rent, so hiring an attorney was out of the question. Besides, I didn't know any.

So when someone came along and said they liked my song well enough to buy it, I never argued price. Or if artists I admired said they would record my song, I wasn't about to ask any questions about ownership or royalties. I figured that, at least in some way, I was being paid in hope. And hope was what kept me going.

NIGHT LIFE

When the evening sun goes down
You will find me hanging round
The night life ain't no good life
But it's my life

Many people just like me
Dreaming of old used-to-be's
And the night life ain't no good life
But it's my life

Listen to the blues they're playing
Listen to what the blues are saying

Mine is just another scene
From the world of broken dreams
And the night life ain't no good life
But it's my life

When I first met Ray Charles, who became one of my best friends, he said, "Willie, I gotta be honest. When I first heard 'Night Life,' I was sure it was written by a Black man."

"Thank you," was my quick reply. It was one of the nicest compliments I've ever received.

The song's been sung by everyone from Aretha Franklin to B.B. King. I like their versions more than my own. It's not because I don't think white people can't sing the blues. They can. I can. But in doing so, I gotta remember the blues is a musical form, even a spiritual form, that originally comes out of the Black struggle. The blues are beautiful because they transform sad to glad. When you sing them, and when you listen to them, you can feel that heavy weight of heartbreak starting to lift.

Did I have the blues as a young man? Hell, I think we're all born with the blues. We get the blues the minute we realize we're gonna die. And no matter how far we evolve in our thinking, the thought of physical annihilation is never a pretty one. We comfort ourselves with thoughts to help energize us in a positive direction. I personally believe in reincarnation. But even though I look forward to slipping into a different form doesn't mean that I'm eager to slip out of this present form.

Yes, night is followed by day. But that new day, for all its golden glory, will, like butter, soon melt into the darkness of night.

FUNNY HOW TIME SLIPS AWAY

Well, hello there
My, it's been a long, long time
How am I doing?
Oh, well, I guess I'm doing fine
It's been so long now and it seems that
It was only yesterday
Gee, ain't it funny how time slips away?

How's your new love?
I hope that he's doing fine
Heard you told him
That you'd love him till the end of time
Well, you know, that's the same thing
That you told me
Well, it seems like just the other day
Gee, ain't it funny how time slips away?

I gotta go now
Guess I'll see you hanging round
Don't know when, though,
Never know when I'll be back in town
But remember what I told you
That in time you're gonna pay
Gee, ain't it surprising how time
  slips away?

Here's the funny part about "Funny How Time Slips Away":

It has. Even though I wrote the damn thing over sixty years ago.

It feels like only yesterday that the story fell out of my brain onto the page. Like all these songs, I let my unconscious do the work.

Maybe my unconscious was thinking of mystery movies. I love those film noirs from the fifties like *Kiss Me Deadly* and *The Big Heat*. Maybe "Funny How Time Slips Away" is a minimovie, with its black widow–type character, a woman who does a man dirty.

Was there such a woman in my life?

Don't think so. If anything, it's been the other way around. I haven't always acted with unquestionable honor.

So why did I create a black widow who hurts a man to the quick?

Simplest answer is that the sultry seductress has been an alluring character ever since Antony hooked up with Cleopatra. Shakespeare wrote a play about them that takes up five acts and will probably be staged till the end of time.

My little song, a far more modest statement, may not enjoy such a long life. If it disappears, that'll be a shame. But what can you do? Songs, like time, do slip away.

CRAZY

I'm crazy, crazy for feeling so lonely
I'm crazy, crazy for feeling so blue

I knew that you'd love me as long as you wanted
And then someday you'd leave me for somebody new

Worry, why do I let myself worry?
Wondering what in the world did I do?

I'm crazy for thinking that my love could hold you
I'm crazy for trying and crazy for crying
And I'm crazy for loving you

Sometimes the craziest stories are the best.

And God knows how many crazy stories have come out of Tootsies Orchid Lounge, the famous barroom in downtown Nashville a few feet from Ryman Auditorium, home to the Grand Ole Opry. I was in there one night and saw Charlie Dick. I knew he was married to sweet Patsy Cline, who sang like an angel. I had a scratchy record of me singing "Crazy" where I sure as hell didn't sound like an angel. I sounded more like a man desperate to have someone else sing the song. Anyway, I played it for Charlie, who liked it so well he drove me over to his house at one a.m., woke up poor Patsy, and made her listen to it.

Because Patsy liked it, I was poor no longer.

It almost didn't happen because Patsy, who recorded it in a Nashville studio, tried singing like me. Big mistake. No one should ever try to follow my style of phrasing. Not that I don't like my style. I do. I believe it's natural, at least for me. But it's offbeat. I tend to kick way back behind the beat or hurry up ahead of the beat. As my good buddy Waylon Jennings once said, "Willie wouldn't know where the beat is if it bit him in the butt."

Fortunately, Patsy's famous producer, Owen Bradley, urged her to forget my phrasing and stick to her own.

Crazy is as crazy does, and this particular "Crazy" convinced me, at a time when I wasn't a hundred percent sure of my writing talent, that I'd be crazy to stop writing.

It doesn't get much more country than the Grand Ole Opry.

I GOTTA GET DRUNK

Well, I gotta get drunk and I sure do dread it
'Cause I know just what I'm gonna do
I'll start to spend my money calling everybody
    honey
And wind up singing the blues
I'll spend my whole paycheck on some old
    wreck
Brother, I can name you a few
Well, I have gotta get drunk and I sure do
    dread it
'Cause I know just what I'm gonna do

I gotta get drunk, I can't stay sober
There's a lot of people in town
That'd like to hear me holler, see me spend my
    dollars
And I wouldn't think of letting 'em down
There's a lot of doctors that tell me
That I'd better start slowing it down
But there's more old drunks than there are old
    doctors
So I guess we better have another round

I've written some stupid songs, and "I Gotta Get Drunk" may be one of them. Stupid, though, doesn't mean bad. A stupid song—about a guy who's about to do something dumb—can be a good song. This is certainly a true song.

True songs are those that paint humans the way they really are. I guess you could call this one a self-portrait of me as an idiot. I was a dumb drinker. Many drinkers are. You might even say most heavy drinkers are. Booze can turn your brain to mush. Only a mush brain would challenge someone twice his size to a fight. Or hit on someone's wife when that someone is standing right there.

In the last part of the song, I sing about doctors' advice to slow down and then add a line that sounds smart: "There's more old drunks than there are old doctors." Except that probably isn't true. It really isn't a smart remark; it's smart-ass.

When I was drinking, I wrote what I was living. I could be a smart-ass. And even today I'm not against smart-ass songs. They're fun. But the bottom line is that, for me, there's nothing funny about drinking. If I hadn't put down the bottle, I'd be dead long ago and never have this chance to write about some of my dumb mistakes.

Hattie Louise "Tootsie" Bess with her whistle at closing time.

THE PARTY'S OVER

Turn out the lights, the party's over
They say that all good things must end
Call it a night, the party's over
And tomorrow starts the same old
   thing again

What a crazy crazy party
Never seen so many people
Laughing, dancing
Look at you, you're having fun

But look at me, I'm almost crying
But that don't keep her love from dying
Misery 'cause for me
The party's over

Turn out the lights, the party's over
They say that all good things must end
Call it a night, the party's over
And tomorrow starts the same old
   thing again

Once I had a love undying
I didn't keep it, wasn't trying
Life for me was just one party
And then another

I broke her heart so many times
Had to have my party wine
And then one day she said
"Sweetheart, the party's over"

You could say that "The Party's Over" is the hangover following "I Gotta Get Drunk." Both songs are soaked in bad booze.

Some people say it's not good to feel sorry for yourself. Maybe so, but when it comes to songwriting, self-pity ain't a bad attitude to embrace. Folks relate. From time to time, we all get to feeling sorry for ourselves.

But how sorry could I feel for myself when, sixteen years after I wrote "The Party's Over," the party wasn't really over after all? The party had just begun.

In the sixties I recorded the song for RCA and it went nowhere. But then in the seventies, my good friend Jerry Wexler signed me to Atlantic and let me sing whatever I wanted. Even better, he trusted me to produce myself. The label underwrote a live album that I cut in Austin's Texas Opry House. I included my party song. That was its first reincarnation.

Then it got born again. Its midwife turned out to be my buddy "Dandy" Don Meredith, the Hall of Fame Dallas Cowboys quarterback turned commentator. Along with Howard Cosell on *Monday Night Football*, Don let you know when the game was out of reach by singing his out-of-tune version of "The Party's Over." I couldn't care less that he was out of tune, especially because he'd tell those millions of football fans that Willie Nelson was the writer and they better go see ol' Willie the next time he comes to their town.

Merle Haggard once told me, "That's the saddest party song ever written."

"Maybe so, Merle," I said, "but there's good money in sadness."

Jerry Wexler, a producer who helped me find my voice, in and out of the studio.

MR. RECORD MAN

Mr. Record Man, I'm looking for a
song I heard today
There was someone blue singing
about someone who went away
Just like me, his heart was yearning
for a love that used to be
It's a lonely song about a lonely man
like me

There was something about a love
that didn't treat him right
And he'd wake from troubled sleep
and cry her name at night
Mr. Record Man, get this record for
me, won't you please?
It's a lonely song about a lonely man
like me

I was driving down the highway
with the radio turned on
And the man that I heard singing
sounded so blue and all alone
As I listened to his lonely song, I
wondered could it be?
Could there somewhere be another
lonely man like me?

Early on, I adopted an attitude that said I could write a song about anything. I could even write a song about a song.

Even more, I could write a song about how I'm *looking* for a song.

"Mr. Record Man" has special meaning because I actually became Mr. Record Man. I worked as a deejay everywhere from Fort Worth, Texas, to Portland, Oregon. I wasn't half bad. I got to shoot the bull and, better yet, got to listen to all the new records coming out. Could be Ray Price. Could be Patti Page or Tennessee Ernie Ford or Chuck Berry or Little Richard or Elvis Presley. I liked them all. I learned from them all.

Appreciating the power of Mr. Record Man was a lesson I learned early on. I could just about play whatever I wanted. Back then things weren't stuck in strict genres the way they are today. Music was music and music always made me happy.

Naming a song "Mr. Record Man" was an act of respect. In a weird way, I was writing a song to myself, even as I was writing it to other deejays out there who I hoped would figure out that the song they were searching for was the same song I was singing.

Trying to read with my sister Bobbie and my daughter Amy.

HELLO WALLS

Hello walls
How'd things go for you today?
Don't you miss her
Since she up and walked away?
And I'll bet you dread to spend
Another lonely night with me
But lonely walls, I'll keep you company

Hello window
Well, I see that you're still here
Aren't you lonely
Since our darlin' disappeared?
Well, look here, is that a teardrop
In the corner of your pane?
Now don't you try to tell me that it's rain

She went away and left us all alone
The way she planned
Guess we'll have to learn to get along
Without her if we can

Hello ceiling
I'm gonna stare at you awhile
You know I can't sleep
So won't you bear with me awhile?
We must all stick together or else
I'll lose my mind
I've got a feeling she'll be gone a long,
    long time

I got my first-ever full-time job as a songwriter outside Nashville on Two Mile Pike. Ray Price, a country music immortal, co-owned the publishing company. The fifty-bucks-a-week salary made me feel rich. I shared an office with my partner, Hank Cochran. One day, when he got called out of our little room to answer the phone—we didn't have a phone of our own—I stared at the walls and the walls talked back. So did the ceiling. So did the window. I scribbled down whatever was coming through me, whether it made sense or not.

By the time Hank got back, the song had written itself.

"You even made a pun," said Hank.

"I did? Where do you see a pun?" I asked.

"The line when you're talking to the window and you say, 'Is that a teardrop in the corner of your pane?' You spelled it 'pane' but could have spelled it 'pain.'"

That's how unsophisticated I was. I had to have my own words explained to me by someone else.

Faron Young, a huge star, liked it. I still needed grocery money and was ready to sell it to him cheap. "I'll loan you the grocery money, Willie," said Faron, "but you keep the song. I don't want to hear you bitching when I turn it into a hit." When Faron did, in fact, turn it into a hit, one of those deejays asked me if I was surprised.

"To be honest," I said, "I'm dumb enough to think everything I write is going to be a hit."

Faron Young and me celebrating a race car named after our song. Judging from its condition, I'm not sure if it's a good or bad thing.

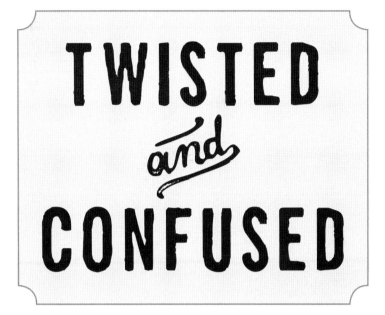

TWISTED and CONFUSED

I'm all for confusion. Confusion is the flip side of perfection. People who think they're perfect—or **want to be perfect**—will never admit to confusion. But, as far as I can see, it's damn near impossible to get through life without being confused. Beyond the big philosophical questions, like "Why does evil exist?" there are little questions, like "Why do I write songs that I don't completely understand?"

Is it okay to be confused by your own songs?

Is it okay to write a song with a twisted message?

I say yes.

And I have some mighty convincing examples to prove my case.

UNDO THE RIGHT

If you can't say you love me say you hate me
And that you regret each time you held me
   tight
If you can't be mine forever then forsake me
If you can't undo the wrong, undo the right

It was right when you loved me only
But wrong when you held another tight
So before you go away and leave me lonely
If you can't undo the wrong, undo the right

It's too late to say your heart is filled
   with sorrow
You can't undo what's done, why do you try?
So please, help me to face the new tomorrows
If you can't undo the wrong, undo the right

A guru with a name I can't remember once said that all wisdom is contained in paradox.

My lifetime paradox is that I take my playing seriously and, at the same time, I don't. After all, I'm just playing around. If I start taking my writing super seriously, I'll get self-conscious and start second-guessing myself.

Same paradox applies to wordplay. It's as serious as it's silly.

If you got a gal who can't love you, it's serious for you to say, "Then go on and hate me." But that's also a silly thing to say, as silly as saying "Undo the right," when the right is what made you happy.

"That's confusing," said Hank Cochran when we wrote the song together during those early Nashville days. I'd written the lyrics and Hank was messing with the music. "Can't you be a little clearer about what you're trying to say, Willie?"

"If I try to straighten out my thoughts," I said, "they won't make sense."

"They don't make sense now," Hank insisted.

"Maybe that'll make folks listen to the song again. Maybe they'll have a good time trying to figure out what's on my mind."

"What *is* on your mind, Willie?"

"Have no idea."

With Hank Cochran. And please don't mistake me for a priest.

SEVEN YEAR ITCH

I had the seven year itch
Scratched it out in three
You may say, "How?"
But you don't know me

I've taken my licks
And I'm paying my fee
I had the seven year itch
Scratched it out in three

Been riding my mind round my neighborhood
Getting nowhere slow but I'm feeling good
Stayed up all night, that's when I'm at my best
Sleep all day and that's too much rest

I went crazy one day
But I came back when
I caught myself going crazy again
I decided to write the world's best song
But when I got around to it
It had done moved on

I had the seven year itch
Scratched it out in three
Well, you may say, "How?"
But you don't know me

I've taken my licks
And I'm paying my fee
I had the seven year itch
Scratched it out in three

I'm a big Marilyn Monroe fan. She was a great comic actor.

Her movie called *The Seven Year Itch* made an impression on me.

There's that famous scene where she's standing on top of the subway grate and the wind causes her dress to billow up.

Was Marilyn on my mind when I wrote my own *Seven Year Itch*?

Probably not, but who knows? I'd like to think so.

The movie is about a married guy who's dying to sleep with Marilyn, the sexiest single lady on the planet, but he's plagued by guilt.

I've had a lifelong relationship with temptation. When it comes to restraint, my track record is not outstanding. But this song, written later in my life, is about a guy who might have found some discipline. He admits he's still yearning. He admits he's crazy. He even admits he's still looking to write the world's best song.

Finally, though, like the horny man chasing Marilyn, he understands that the harder you try, the further the prize slips away.

Oscar Wilde, the witty nineteenth-century writer with world-class credentials, had a different point of view. He wrote that "the only way to get rid of a temptation is to yield to it."

But that attitude got Oscar into trouble.

I've had trouble of my own—which is why I decided to reduce the seven years to three.

COME ON BACK JESUS

Come on back Jesus
And pick up John Wayne on the way

The world's done gone crazy
And it seems to get worse every day
So come on back Jesus
And pick up John Wayne on the way

Time to take off the gloves
They just don't respect peace anymore
But if we have old John Wayne
We know he can swing from the floor

While he kicks their butts
We'll just stand there and watch him and pray
So come on back Jesus
And pick up John Wayne on the way

It's getting real hairy
If only old duke man was here
He'd blow them evil bastards
From out past the atmosphere

Lord, the news looked so scary
When I glanced at the paper today
So come on back Jesus
And pick up John Wayne on the way

According to my handy dictionary, "sarcasm" is defined as "a cutting, often ironic remark intended to give pain."

Which brings me to the question: Are sarcastic songs meant to hurt anyone?

I don't think so. When Buddy Cannon, my son Micah, and I were fooling around with the song that became "Come On Back Jesus," we weren't looking to harm a soul. We were just poking a little fun at what seemed to be a prominent attitude in some versions of organized religion.

I have nothing against John Wayne. I love cowboy movies and even made a few myself. Cowboys were my first heroes.

And naturally I love America and the American people.

I was born a Christian and described Jesus as Perfect Man, someone who tried to teach us to live life through love.

It's just that Jesus, unlike my beloved cowboys, didn't fight back. As best as I can read the Bible, violence wasn't his thing.

So if he's coming back and bringing The Duke with him, that would be downright surprising. It would be a good joke, which is as good a definition of this song as any.

Are sarcastic songs meant to hurt anyone?

THE SOUND IN YOUR MIND

I've been feeling a little bad
Because I've been feeling a little
   better without you
It's a little like rain but it's a lot like
   a sunny day

And it's hard to explain
But the sound of your name don't make
   music anymore
It's more than a sound of a love that
   I lost one day

It's a little too late to start thinking
   about starting all over
I'd rather stay where I am
I can't take another slam in the mind

I've been feeling a little bad
'Cause I've been feeling a little better
   without you
But remember my love is the sound that
   you hear in your mind

I've been running around even laughing
   at half of the memories
And you're not hard to remember
I just have to think of your name

It was the mid-seventies. Springtime in Austin. I was jogging with a friend around Town Lake, that beautiful body of water in the middle of the city. After a couple of miles, we took a break.

Sitting on a bench, I looked up. The sky couldn't be bluer. Flowers were blooming. Birds were singing.

"I'm hurting, Willie," said my pal.

"From what?" I asked.

"My little darling up and left me last night."

"Sorry to hear that, buddy."

"But the sorriest part is that I'm feeling bad for feeling good about it."

"Then you wanted her gone?"

"If you'd asked me that yesterday, I'd say no."

"But today you're okay?"

"Today I keep wondering if I chased her away."

I didn't know what to say, so I said nothing. The silence stayed until my friend got up and sighed.

"I'm hearing something," he said, "but I don't know what it is."

"That's just the sound in your mind."

"'The sound in your mind,'" he repeated. "Sounds like a song."

When I got home and found myself scribbling words on a yellow pad, I saw that my buddy was right.

Running and moving have helped me live a long life. And you have to do that with style.

LOCAL MEMORY

The lights go out each evening at eleven
And up and down our block there's not a sound
I close my eyes and search for peaceful slumber
And just then the local memory comes around

Piles of blues against the door to make sure
    sleep will come no more
She's the hardest-working memory in this town
Turns out happiness again, then lets loneliness
    back in
And each night the local memory comes around

Each day I say tonight I may escape her
I pretend I'm happy and never even frown
But at night I close my eyes and pray sleep finds
    me
But again the local memory comes around

Rids the house of all good news, then sets out
    my crying shoes
What a faithful memory, never lets me down
We're both up till light of day chasing happiness
    away
And each night the local memory comes around

My older sister Bobbie
was a beautiful anchor
in my life.

I don't usually remember my dreams, but sometimes I do. And when I do, I realize the power of creativity. When I go over the scenes of the dreams, I'm amazed that my mind can make up such amazing stuff.

One dream found its way into a song. I call it a local dream because I was back in my hometown of Abbott, Texas, population 300. I was sitting on the porch of the home of Doc Simms, the man who delivered both me and my big sister Bobbie in that very house. In real life, after my career was in good shape and the good doctor had died, I bought his place and moved in for a while. But in this dream Doc was still alive. Inside he was seeing patients while I was outside sitting in a rocking chair and playing my guitar.

I played all afternoon until the sun started to set. I watched the sky turn from gold to pink to purple. As night descended, I kept on playing. The light from a full moon lit the fields of cotton and corn across the way. There wasn't a soul in sight.

The song I was playing was sad. I had lost something, but I didn't know what it was. It wasn't money. It wasn't anything material. It was an emotion that felt like love. More than an emotion, it was a memory that I couldn't bring to life. I realized there was only one way to capture the memory: I had to keep playing.

As I played, the night turned misty. I saw the memory creeping back. It was shrouded in fog. But it had a form. A human form. It was a woman.

"What's your name?" I asked her.

"Just call me Memory," she said. "Local Memory is my name."

ONE IN A ROW

If you can truthfully say
That you've been true just one day
Well, that makes one in a row
One in a row, one in a row

And if you can look into my eyes
One time without telling lies
Well, that makes one in a row
One in a row, one in a row

Why do I keep loving you
After all the things you do?

And just one time come into my arms
And be glad that you're in my arms
That will make one in a row
One in a row, one in row

"But do I get to sing any
of my own songs?"

This is a song from the sixties. It came out on an RCA album that was another unsuccessful attempt to turn me into a singing star when I was still mainly known for writing.

I didn't care for the title, *Make Way for Willie Nelson*, because I didn't like a label giving out orders to the fans. The fans would make way for me when they were good and ready. And while I was still tooling around Nashville, they still weren't quite ready. Anyway, in those days I was holding back my rebellious spirit in the hope that going along with the label's program would get me somewhere.

My producer was a good man named Felton Jarvis. He was producing Elvis—and would continue to do so for ten years—while producing me. It was hard for me to argue with someone of his stature.

On this particular album, he insisted that I sing songs written by other people. I didn't mind, especially when Felton suggested "A Mansion on the Hill," the Hank Williams/Fred Rose classic.

"But do I get to sing any of my own songs?" I asked Felton.

"You can choose one, Willie," he said.

"Well, that's one in a row."

"You have the song written?" he wanted to know.

"I do now."

GOOD HEARTED WOMAN

A long time forgotten are dreams that just fell
by the way
The good life he promised ain't what she's
living today

But she never complains of the bad times or
bad things he's done
She just talks about the good times they've had
and all the good times to come

She's a good hearted woman in love with a
good timing man
She loves him in spite of his ways she don't
understand

Through teardrops and laughter they'll pass
through this world hand in hand
A good hearted woman loving her good timing
man

He likes the bright lights and night life and
good timing friends
And when the party's all over she'll welcome
him back home again

Lord knows she don't understand him, but she
does the best that she can
This good hearted woman is loving a good
timing man

It's about time to talk about poker, a game that's captivated me for much of my life.

"Good Hearted Woman" came out of one game I was playing with Waylon Jennings, along with some other buddies, in a Fort Worth motel on the notorious Jacksboro Highway. It was one of those all-night games that, when it was over, left us all blurry eyed. I have no recollection of whether I won or lost.

But I do remember Waylon, who had the energy of a steam engine, saying, "Willie, we're done playing but we're not done writing. I've got this song with a missing part that needs filling in. Will you help me?"

"Sing it," I said.

Waylon picked up his guitar and sang it strong. I knew right away it was about him and Jessi Colter, the love of his life.

"Sounds like you got it under control, Waylon."

"But what about that missing line?"

I suggested a line that said, "Through teardrops and laughter we're gonna walk through the world hand in hand."

"That's it!" Waylon shouted. "That's perfect! I'm giving you half the song."

I protested—it was too much—but got overruled. Waylon was a great guy whose generosity paid off a hundredfold when he included us singing the song on *Wanted! The Outlaws*, the first country album to sell over a million copies.

LADY LUCK

The winners tell jokes and the losers say deal
Lady Luck rides a stallion tonight

And she smiles at the winners and she
    laughs at the losers
And the losers say that just ain't right

But they keep right on playing and paying
    and praying
That someday their luck just might change

And if you're surveying the table and you're
    looking for the sucker
Oh by the way, sir, what is your name?

Lady Luck rides a stallion tonight

I'll bet you a hundred if you've still got a
    hundred
One more wager, winner take all

'Cause sweet Lady Luck likes me a lot more
    than you
And I'm betting she'll come when I call

When the loser has no more to bet
And the winner wants all he can get

Lady Luck will go riding off in the moonlight
Lady Luck rides a stallion tonight

Let's keep talking about poker.

I put this "Lady Luck" on a recent album called *God's Problem Child*. Not that I saw my love for poker as a problem. I see it more as a pleasure. Maybe a pleasure I've overindulged, but a pleasure nonetheless.

For that pleasure I must thank the late great Zeke Varnon, a fun-loving man I met when I was just out of high school. Recently home from the army, Zeke was the sort of rogue that added spice to life in small-town Texas. He was a drinker, bootlegger, ladies' man, and world-class gambler. He was the first guy to paint a portrait of Lady Luck that stuck with me from then till now.

"She'll make you think you're special," said Zeke. "She'll smile, she'll wink, she'll whisper sweet nothings in your ear. She'll act like she's yours and no one else's. She'll get you acting bold. And then, instead of letting you screw her, she'll screw you."

"So how am I supposed to handle her?" I asked.

"Act like she ain't there."

"But she is, isn't she?"

"Only to deceive you. To keep you from studying the other players. Your job, Willie, is to understand them, not her. You'll never figure her out."

I took Zeke's advice to heart, although, being susceptible to willing women, I've sometimes fallen back into the trap of thinking that she's mine-all-mine.

Which is why I put her on a stallion and had her go riding off to tempt some other fool.

Dolly Parton joins me and the Family for a quick photo
on the set of her show, *Dolly!*

WHY DO I HAVE TO CHOOSE

Why do I have to choose
To see everybody lose
To walk around and sing the blues
Well, darling, I refuse

Love is hard to find
Love of any kind
And a love like yours and mine
Creates its own design

And when I think of her
And then I think of you
The love is not the same
But either love is true

Why do I have to choose
To see everybody lose
To walk around and sing the blues
Well, darling, I refuse

A song about romantic bewilderment. What better way to conclude this section of "Twisted & Confused"?

I first sang it on my own in the early eighties. A few years later, while I was making an album with Merle Haggard, *Seashores of Old Mexico*, we decided to do it as a duet. Merle really liked the song.

"I like it because it's perverted," he said.

"Is that like calling me a pervert?" I asked.

"Nope. What I mean by perverted is that you start it out as nothing but another love song. You're singing to your gal. While she's listening to it, she's got to be loving it. You're telling her there ain't no love like the love between you and her."

"Well, there's nothing wrong with that."

"Except you pull out the rug from under her. You bring another woman into the picture. That's how you pervert your love song. You start out sweet and then go sour. And what's worse, you don't let either one know what you're gonna do. You're breaking two hearts at once."

"Well, that's my choice. But if it's so perverse, why do you wanna sing it, Merle?"

"'Cause I'll be singing the story of my life."

You start out sweet and then go sour.

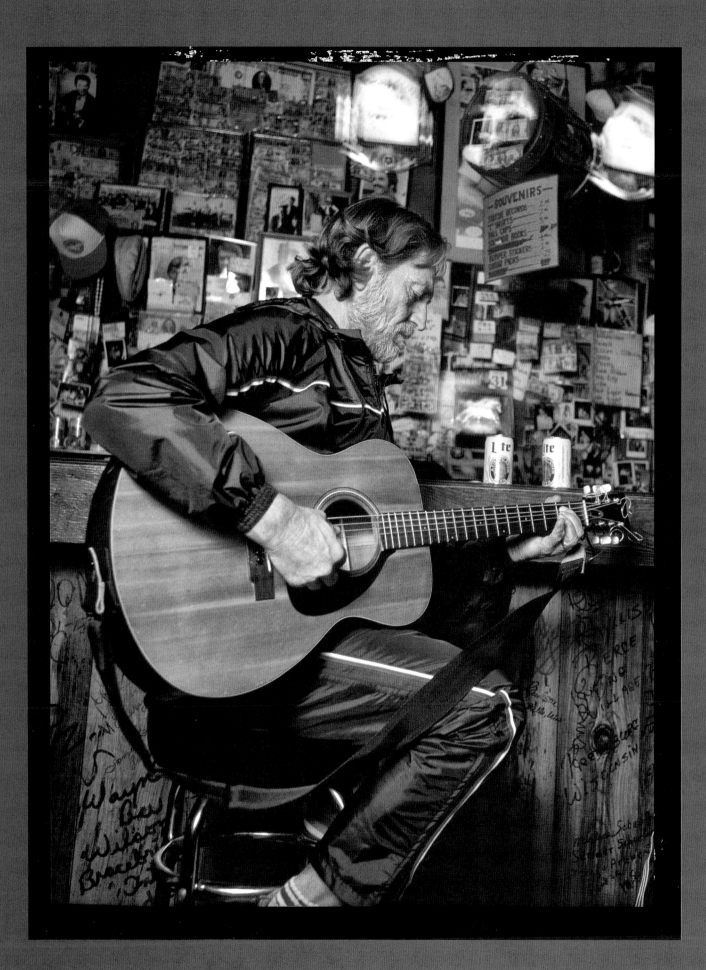

HALF a MAN

Sometimes we get the idea that our job, whether big or small, is complete. For example, we decide to write a book and after the final chapter type out THE END. Except a week later we remember a bunch of important stuff that we left out. We mow the grass and the next day we notice a big patch we missed. We fall in love and give ourselves over to the object of affection only to realize—a day or a week or a year later—that we've been holding back.

Completion is an illusion.

We're all works in progress. The minute you stop growing, you stop living.

I see my songs the same way. When I read them over, many of them only half express what I wanted to say. But that's okay. They're reflections of little moments in time. I consider them more like questions than answers.

When the light's red, you stop at the curb. When it turns green, you walk across. My songs are like green lights. It's okay to walk across. But just don't dillydally, because the light's fixing to turn red again.

HALF A MAN

If I'd only had one arm to hold you
Better yet if I had none at all
Then I wouldn't have two arms that
  ache for you
That'd be one less memory to recall

If I only had one ear to listen
To the lies that you told to me
Then I would more closely resemble
The half a man that you've made of me

And if I had been born with but one eye
And then only had one eye to cry
And if half of my heart turned to ashes
Maybe half of my heartaches
  would die

And if I only had one leg to stand on
Then a much truer picture you'd see
Then I'd more closely resemble
The half a man that you've made of me

JULY 1962

I was in Las Vegas on my honeymoon with my second wife, Shirley Collie, a superb singer. She was sleeping on my right arm. I wanted to smoke and, not wanting to disturb her, reached around with my left arm to grab a cigarette off the nightstand. Suddenly the thought came to me, "If I'd only had one arm to hold you . . ."

It was a strange thought that got me in an anatomical frame of mind. Piece by piece, I started amputating myself. I cut out an ear, I cut out an eye, I cut out a leg. It all felt morbid. But morbid isn't a bad mood for songs. I remembered reading something Alfred Hitchcock said about his movies: "Give them pleasure. The same pleasure they have when they wake up from a nightmare."

Rather than take myself apart, I saw my woman taking me apart. That was a little bit more lurid.

Now I can understand if you're thinking that's a strange song for someone to write on his own honeymoon. But the truth is that when I sang it for Shirley, she liked it and sang along with me.

Years later, my good friend Joe Jamail, a prominent personal injury attorney, represented a man who'd lost his arm in a car accident. In his closing argument, Joe recited the lyrics to "Half a Man." He told me that many of the jurors wept. Then the defendant wept when the jury came back with a humongous payoff for Joe's client.

THE WORDS DON'T FIT THE PICTURE

If this is a game we play
And if this is a role I play
Where are the words I say to you
The words don't fit the picture anymore

And if we've been acting all along
And we both act right and we both act wrong
Where does it say that we should cry
It's just the words don't fit the picture anymore

The words don't fit the picture anymore
No need to force the love scenes anymore

And a one-act play comes to an end
And as we turn to leave we can both part friends
But this is the time to say goodbye
'Cause the words don't fit the picture anymore

Picture this:

The woman stands at the kitchen counter. Her back is to her man. She says, "I was thinking of you today."

The man is sitting at the table. He's playing solitaire. He says, "I was thinking of you too."

The woman washes a plate. She still doesn't bother to turn around. She says, "I like the idea of you thinking of me."

The man is still absorbed in his card game. He says, "I feel the same."

"If I could read your mind," asks the woman as she puts the dishes in the cupboard, "what would I learn?"

The man turns a card over, but there's nowhere to put it. He says, "You wouldn't learn much. What's on your mind?"

She says, "Nothing."

That night before going to bed, they don't bother to kiss. She's thinking of someone else. So is he.

She says, "I love you, darling."

He says, "I love you too."

They sleep on opposite sides of the bed.

The words don't fit the picture.

She's thinking of someone else.
So is he.

WHAT CAN YOU DO TO ME NOW?

What can you do to me now
That you haven't done to me already?
You broke my pride and made me
   cry out loud
What can you do to me now?

I'm seeing things that I never thought
   I'd see
You've opened up the eyes inside of me
How long have you been doing this to me
I'm seeing sides of me that I can't believe

Someway somehow I'll make a man of me
I will build me back the way I used to be
Much stronger now the second time around
'Cause what can you do to me now?

Can songs prophesize?

Maybe.

In December of 1970, my partner Hank Cochran and I were on a writing streak. We were in the basement of my house on Greer Road in Ridgetop, thirty miles east of Nashville—I had seventeen acres of rich red-clay Tennessee soil—and cranking out one tune after another. By the time we got through writing the seventh song, we decided to stop.

"I'm thinking at least one of these suckers is bound to be a hit," I said.

"I'm thinking all of them," said Hank, who heartily shook my hand and went on his way.

Next evening, I drove into Nashville for a Christmas party at the King of the Road hotel, owned by Roger Miller, who wrote the song that carried its name. I was having a relaxing time with a bunch of cronies when someone called me to the phone. It was my nephew.

"Uncle Willie," he said. "Your house is on fire."

By the time I rushed home, all I could do was save my guitar Trigger and some primo weed. The house burned to the ground.

It was only then that I thought of the seventh song that Hank and I had written only hours earlier.

Whenever I sing "What Can You Do to Me Now?" I still the feel the heat from the furious flames.

"Your house is on fire."

YOU LEFT A LONG, LONG TIME AGO

You tell me today that you're leaving
But just think a while, I'm sure that you
　must know
Today might be the day that you walk away
But you left me a long, long time ago

Today is just the day that ends it all
Except the usual memories that always
　linger on
And today might be the day that you walk
　away
But you left me a long, long time ago

I stood with helpless hands and watched me
　lose your love
A little more each day then it was gone
I kept wondering just how long until this day
　would come
How long could your pride keep hanging on

So please don't say you're sorry, don't say
　anything
Don't try to say why you must leave, just go
And today might be the day that you
　walk away
But you left me a long, long time ago

If couples therapy had been popular when I was coming up as a songwriter, I might not have a career.

I've called this chapter "Half a Man" because half of the time when romance goes sour, at least one half of the couple doesn't know why. Things remain unsaid. Dirt pushed under the rug. Warnings ignored. I should know. I've done more than my fair share of ignoring warnings. The words "ignoring" and "ignorance" are kissing cousins.

Thanks to Dolly Parton, I got to act out the story I made up in "You Left a Long, Long Time Ago." Dolly invited me and Brenda Lee to sing it as a duet on her TV show. Brenda came up with a good approach. She said, "Let's be sitting at a table and acting like we're trying to communicate. Only as you're there singing the song and playing your guitar, I'll be reading a newspaper, as if I don't care. Will that bother you?"

"Yes," I said, "and that's why we should do it."

"Maybe, just to be civil, Willie, I'll look up and give you a fleeting glance."

"Okay, but how are we going to end the thing?" I asked.

"When we're through singing, you get up and walk away in one direction and I'll wander off in another."

Perfect.

They tell me that you can catch this little one-act play on YouTube. Might be fun to sneak a peek to see what this old guitar picker looked like a long, long time ago.

WONDERFUL FUTURE

Today as I walk through my garden
  of dreams
I'm alone in the sweet used-to-be
My past and my present are one and
  the same
And the future holds nothing for me

Yesterday's kisses still burning
Yesterday's memories still find me
Scenes from the past keep returning
I've got a wonderful future behind me

You say there is happiness waiting for me
But I know this is just fantasy
Let me trade one tomorrow for one yesterday
Let me live in my garden of dreams

Yesterday's kisses still burning
Yesterday's memories still find me
Scenes from the past keep returning
I've got a wonderful future behind me

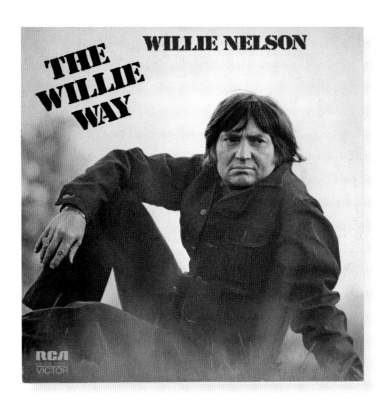

Been fifty-one years since this song came out on *The Willie Way*, **the same album where I sang** *"You Left a Long, Long Time Ago."* In the cover photo I'm wearing a denim jacket and a scowl that looks like I've just lost my last friend.

Looking at that picture now, I'm trying to remember whether that particular shot was chosen by me or someone at the label. Doesn't really matter. It's a reflection of a mood that, if only for a fleeting second, caught something I was feeling.

I claim that I separate myself from my songs. I say that as a storyteller I make up stories that most of the time have nothing to do with me. It's pure invention. But nothing is completely pure. If pessimism wasn't part of my normally optimistic outlook, it wouldn't keep cropping up in my music.

The optimist looks forward. The optimist says the future is wonderful. The pessimist looks backward. The pessimist says those good days are long gone. The argument is ongoing. The tension is painful. The resolution is nowhere in sight.

So how does the man with the scowl on his face handle the dilemma?

He wants to write something beautiful and sweet. He wants to write about happiness. He wants to inspire the world and give everyone reason to hope. But he also wants to be honest. And since he is a walking contradiction, honesty requires that he write a song that holds two truths at once. It's only when that song is written that his scowl might turn into a smile. That's doubly true when he sings the song in front of a crowd of people. Their smiles tell him that they relate. He sees how the song simultaneously reflects and deflects the pain of love.

AMNESIA

I guess I can't write anymore
I guess I got no more to say
Or else I'd be putting it down
Instead of just throwing it away

I work like a slave for the future
And gave everything that I love to the past
There's a whole string of Septembers that I can't remember
and I hope my amnesia will last

Why should I remember what's in it for me
Will I live longer and will I be stronger
Why should I return to the past
Lord, I hope my amnesia will last

In order to remember,
you have to forget.

It's only right that I can't remember having written a song called "Amnesia." My sister Bobbie, whose memory was better than mine, had to remind me about it.

When we recorded it on the Willie/Bobbie album called *December Day: Willie's Stash Volume 1*, damn if I hadn't forgotten one of the three verses! By the time I sang it on the TV show *Austin City Limits*, I managed to remember those lost lines and was finally able to sing the thing in its entirety.

The origin of what some might call a half-assed song was simple:

I hadn't written for a long while. Normally, unproductive periods don't bother me. After I've turned out a song, I often feel like that might be the last thing I'll ever write. That usually doesn't sweat me, but this time it did. This time I didn't like the idea of having no ideas. I got a little nervous. Maybe my brain was drained. Maybe I'd said everything I had to say. Maybe this was a permanent block. I racked my brain for a solution and, praise be the forces of creativity, I came up with one:

I'd write about having nothing to write about.

Turned out to be easy. It was a story about not having a story. But in writing that story, a new element came into play: the business of amnesia. I started thinking how amnesia, usually considered a negative, might be a positive.

In order to remember, you have to forget. The more we forget, the more memories come to mind. And each memory contains the seed of a song.

Bottom line: I'm glad I forgot about "Amnesia" and look forward to doing a whole lot more forgetting.

LAYING MY BURDENS DOWN

I used to walk stooped
From the weight of my tears
But I just started laying my burdens down

I used to duck bullets from the rifle of fear
But I just started laying my burdens down

Oh, I'm laying 'em down
But I just started laying my burdens down

The flesh ain't nothing but the bark on the tree
I just started laying my burdens down
The tree isn't nothing but the soul in me

My soul took love on a hell of a ride
I just started laying my burdens down
My soul ain't nothing but the car love drives

Love said, "Mama, can I come on home?"
I just started laying my burdens down
And God said, "Son, you ain't never been gone"
I just started laying my burdens down

I'll do my best to end this "Half a Man" chapter on a less confusing note.

This song came from a time when I dealt with my thoughts the only way I knew how: I tried working them out in a song.

It was written back in the sixties, in the RCA days when my producer was Felton Jarvis, who loved working up big productions. When I brought him "Laying My Burdens Down," he saw it as a church song and brought in a choir to raise the roof.

"It's a hymn, but a weird one, Willie," said Jarvis. "I can't believe how many metaphors you put in there."

"Metaphor" was another one of those words I didn't know how to spell, much less understand.

"'Duck bullets from the rifle of fear,'" quoted Felton. "'Flesh is nothing but the bark on the tree.' Those are metaphors, son. You might want to make the language a little simpler so no one gets confused."

"Saying I'm laying my burdens down is pretty darned simple."

"Just a suggestion. What do you say, Willie?"

"I say if it ain't broke, don't fix it."

And I didn't.

YESTERDAY'S WINE

Yesterday's Wine has been called the first concept album in the history of country music. The truth is that I never entertained the concept of a concept album. I just had a bunch of songs that hung together. Looking back, I saw that, taken as a whole, they laid out a landscape much broader than anything I'd done before.

I cut the record over a couple of days at the RCA Nashville Sound studio in May of 1971. I was in a midlife meditative mood. I'd always loved reading and decided to check out various books. As a child in rural Texas, I was introduced to the Bible by the loving people who raised me, my paternal grandparents. I was so fascinated by the book that I wound up teaching it in Sunday school as an adult. Several nontraditional writers and thinkers also touched my heart: Kahlil Gibran, author of *The Prophet*; Edgar Cayce, a mystic healer; and Father A. A. Taliaferro, an Episcopal priest preaching modern mysticism who, like Norman Vincent

In the wake
of silence
I realize it's
my job to
keep singing.

Peale, was all about positive thought. Father Taliaferro's creed was "Learn that you may teach."

Predictably, RCA didn't love the album. Matter of fact, they hated it. Their opinion didn't bother or sway me. The record felt right to me. I succeeded in expressing the feelings running through me. I saw those songs as necessities. They let me think out loud.

Its failure to sell soured my relationship with the label. Wasn't long after that RCA dropped me from their roster. I still didn't care. I figured I could always make a living working barrooms and honky-tonks.

Ironically, *Yesterday's Wine* proved successful with critics even though sales were slim. It took years, but the album came to be recognized as a breakthrough. At the time, I didn't see it that way. I was just putting one foot ahead of the other. As it turned out, I was venturing into new territory. But it wasn't boldness or bravery that drove me; it was a need to reflect on questions that didn't have easy answers.

WHERE'S THE SHOW / LET ME BE A MAN

Explain again to me, Lord, why I'm here
I don't know, I don't know
The setting for the stage is still not clear
Where's the show, where's the show

Let it begin, let it begin
I am born, can you use me

What would you have me to do, Lord
Shall I sing them a song
I could tell them all about you, Lord
I could write of the loves I have known

I'll work in their cotton and corn fields
I promise to do all I can
I'll laugh and I'll cry, I'll live and I'll die
Please, Lord, let me be a man

Dear Lord, let me be a man
And I'll give it all that I can
If I'm needed in this distant land
Please, Lord, let me be a man

Before I begin this elaborate journey
Portraying earth's typical man
Last-minute instructions would surely be welcome
Please, Lord, let me hold to your hand

I start out praying. I start assuming that Perfect Man, whom I was taught to call Jesus, has visited this earth. Since then, God has chosen to be invisible and inaudible. That leaves me a little confused. It leaves me looking for answers.

As a show businessman, I want the show to start. I'll accept the role of Imperfect Man who does what needs to be done.

As a kid, I didn't mind working the cotton and corn fields. That had me toiling shoulder to shoulder with African Americans and Mexicans. They saw me—just as I saw them—as brothers.

Now, though, I'm grown and, wanting to continue to serve the forces of good, I'll go on this journey. I'll follow this cycle of songs to wherever it leads. At the same time, I wouldn't mind some instructions.

The answer to my prayer is silence, and in the wake of silence I realize it's my job to keep singing.

IN GOD'S EYES

Never think evil thoughts of anyone
It's just as wrong to think as to say
For a thought is but a word that's unspoken
In God's eyes he sees it this way

Lend a hand if you can to a stranger
Never worry if he can't repay
For in time you'll be repaid ten times over
In God's eyes he sees it this way

In God's eyes we're like sheep in a meadow
Now and then a lamb goes astray
But open arms should await its returning
In God's eyes he sees it this way

I find myself drawn back to my childhood and lessons learned under the watchful eye of my grandmother, Mama Nelson.

Her faith was steely. Her faith was also simple. God is good. God is love. Love with all your might. Love everyone and everything.

The deep thinkers I had been reading—whether Norman Vincent Peale or Father Taliaferro—added fuel to that faith by reminding me of the power of the mind. The heart feels, but the mind thinks. The Bible combines those elements in Proverbs 23:7 by saying, "As he thinketh in his heart, so is he."

But even if a bad thought leads us astray, we can, like the prodigal son, return to spirit. Spirit will always embrace us. The essence of spirit—loving spirit, positive spirit—is acceptance. Forgiveness and acceptance are linked like mother and child. The bond is unbreakable.

I was thirty-eight years old when I wrote these songs, only to discover that my inner eight-year-old was sitting beside me.

My grandparents, Mama and Daddy Nelson.

FAMILY BIBLE

There's a family Bible on the table
Its pages worn and hard to read
But the family Bible on the table
Will ever be my key to memories

At the end of day when work was over
And when the evening meal was done
Dad would read to us from the family Bible
And we'd count our many blessings
   one by one

I can see us sitting round the table
When from the family Bible Dad would read
I can hear my mother softly singing
"Rock of ages, rock of ages cleft for me"

Now this old world of ours is filled with
   troubles
This old world would oh so better be
If we'd found more Bibles on the tables
And mothers singing "Rock of ages,
   cleft for me"

"Family Bible," though an integral part of *Yesterday's Wine*, was written fourteen years earlier in 1957, when I was a deejay in Vancouver.

I could have placed it in the "Fifty Bucks a Song" chapter because I sold it cheap to get it recorded by Claude Gray. His version was my first hit. A song about faith gave me the faith to move to Nashville, where, in the sixties, I found my footing as a songwriter.

I never recorded the tune, though, until *Yesterday's Wine*. It seemed perfectly suited to this story about a flawed man looking for his place in a flawed world.

The Bible is the most read, most analyzed, and maybe most misused book in world history. Wars have been waged in its name. You can interpret it a million ways. But my approach came from Mama Nelson. She called it the Good Book.

Being a quizzical child, I asked her, "Why is it good?"

"Because," she answered without hesitation, "it teaches you to love."

IT'S NOT FOR ME TO UNDERSTAND

I passed a home the other day
The yard was filled with kids at play
And on the sidewalk of this home
A little boy stood all alone

His smiling face was sweet and kind
But I could see the boy was blind
He listened to the children play
I bowed my head and there I prayed

Dear Lord above, why must this be
And then these words came down to me
After all, you're just a man
And it's not for you to understand

It's not for you to reason why
You too are blind without my eyes
So question not what I command
Because it's not for you to understand

Now when I pray my prayer is one
I pray his will, not mine be done
After all, I'm just a man
And it's not for me to understand

Humility is hard to come by. That's because all of us have unique talents.

When these talents—whether for writing or farming, skateboarding or scientific research—start to bloom, we get excited. Our egos blow up. Our heads get bloated with notions of glory. We think we got it all figured out.

We don't. No one does. The mystery of human life, the dance between good and evil, is unfathomable. Why do so many bad people prosper while good ones starve? Why are innocent children afflicted with disease? Why does power accrue to self-serving leaders dead set on brutality?

It helps to be humble. Helps to understand that I don't have to understand. Helps to know the difference between willpower and willfulness. I have the willpower to keep working at my craft. But the moment I get willful and decide that the world must bend my way, I get out of joint and find myself floundering.

Faith has to do with surrendering to a will not your own. That's the silent will of the universe, in which there is a divine order that we can intuit but can never explain.

It's the still, quiet voice living inside a song that remains unsung.

THESE ARE DIFFICULT TIMES / REMEMBER THE GOOD TIMES

These are difficult times
Lord, please give me a sign
For these are difficult times

Remember the good times
They're smaller in number and
   easier to recall
Don't spend too much time on the
   bad times
Their staggering number will be
   heavy as lead on your mind

Don't waste a moment unhappy
Invaluable moments gone with the
   leakage of time
As we leave on our own separate
   journeys
Moving west with the sun to a place
   buried deep in our minds

My friend Zeke, as wild as he was, liked to philosophize.

"What takes a wise guy an hour to say," he explained, "a wise man can say in a minute." That's one of the reasons I keep my songs short.

I've never been one to overexplain, especially since I'm not sure I have a handle on the right explanation.

I know that reflection is real. We do it all the time. We think back to all those instances where we messed up. Regret becomes automatic, even addictive. Like lead, regret weighs us down.

Reflection on happier times in the past leads to happier times in the present. Reflecting on the future usually brings up apprehension and fear. So, if we're going back in time, I say go back to the good times.

I remember the year 1939 when my grandfather, only fifty-six, caught pneumonia and died within a week. I also remember two months before he passed, when a box arrived in the mail from Sears, Roebuck. I feverishly unwrapped the package. Inside was a surprise that my grandparents had ordered especially for me: a Stella guitar. I was six years old. I put the instrument in my arms and started to strum. Right then and there, Grandpa gave me my first guitar lesson. Eighty-four years later, I envision the scene as though it happened yesterday: Grandpa is alive. My little heart is bursting with joy. The guitar has a wordless voice that comforts me as much now as it did then.

Performing with my longtime bassist Bee Spears and Mickey Raphael on harmonica.

SUMMER OF ROSES

A short time I have to be with you, my love
But a short time is better than no time, you see
So I bring to you all my possessions
And would that you'd share them with me

I bring you one springtime of robins
One springtime of robins to sing
I bring you one summer of roses
One summer of roses I bring

I bring you one autumn of dry leaves
Dry leaves will be helpful you know
To soften the fall of your snowflakes
When I bring you your winter of snow

Does a love song belong in the middle of a metaphysical meditation?

Maybe that question is too fancy. Maybe it's better to ask a simpler question:

Have I ever been able to avoid putting a love song on any of my albums?

Hell, no.

When it comes to spirituality as well as women, I'm a believer. I believe that just as spirit has kept me sane, so have women. Of course, I must add that women have also made me a little insane—but that's on me, not them.

A scholar friend of mine says that in Dante's *Divine Comedy*, a poem some consider the greatest ever written, the poet can only get to God through the guidance of Beatrice, the love of his life. I get it. Romantic love is heavenly. When you're in love with the woman of your dreams, love is no longer an abstract form. It's real as rain.

Because I'm into my ninetieth year, a lot of people want to know my strategy for survival. I don't have an easy answer. Good genes are a matter of good luck. Replacing booze with pot surely gave me many extra years. Swapping out smoking pot with eating edibles helped me strengthen my lungs.

But sticking with love—romantic love, spiritual love, every sort of genuine love—even when it didn't seem like love was sticking with me, may be the key. Love is the elixir that cleanses worldly toxins. I can sing about whiskey and weed, I can cry the blues from here to Houston and back, but it's those love songs that anchor me. Without those love songs, I'm a lost soul. With them, I can feel my heart healing, giving me hope for a better day.

DECEMBER DAY

This looks like a December day
This looks like a time-to-remember day
And I remember a spring, such a sweet tender thing
And love's summer college
Where the green leaves of knowledge
Were waiting to fall with the fall

And where September wine
Numbed a measure of time
Through the tears of October, now November's over
And this looks like a December day

It looks like we've come to the end of the way
And as my memories race back to love's eager beginning
Reluctant to play with the thoughts of the ending
The ending that won't go away
And this looks like a December day

Love has its seasons. Love is transitory. It can last long or be short-lived. Either way, when it's happening—when spring turns to summer and autumn yields to winter—when you look into the eyes of another and see that warm flow and feel, all is right with the world.

Even in the dark season of stone-cold December, when love is frozen over, I'm one of the guys who's willing to wait for the thaw. Melting is magical.

"The sky's covered over with clouds," Mama Nelson used to say, "but the sun hasn't gone anywhere. The sun stays steady. It's the clouds who come and go."

As I sing about an "ending that won't go away," I'm thinking about writing another song that says there's always a new beginning.

I love the way Kahlil Gibran put it:

"When you reach the end of what you should know, you will be at the beginning of what you should sense."

"It's the clouds who come and go."

YESTERDAY'S WINE

Miracles appear in the strangest of places
Fancy meeting you here
The last time I saw you was just out of Houston
Let me sit down and buy you a beer

Your presence is welcome with me and my friend here
This is a hangout of mine
We come here quite often and listen to music
Partaking of yesterday's wine

Yesterday's wine, I'm yesterday's wine
Aging with time like yesterday's wine
Yesterday's wine, we're yesterday's wine
Aging with time like yesterday's wine

You give the appearance of one widely traveled
I'll bet you've seen things in your time
So sit down beside me and tell me your story
If you think you'll like yesterday's wine

So what's happened to our Imperfect Man wandering through the highways and byways of life?

He's prayed, he's stayed focused on some thorny theological questions, he's reflected on romance, and now he's stumbled into a barroom with a friend.

The friend remains unnamed—as does the person who, by chance, he meets. It isn't clear whether it's a he or a she. All we know is that it's a chance encounter. And also a chance to sing a theme song that, I'm afraid, doesn't make the theme much clearer.

And yet it was my choice to title this little suite of songs *Yesterday's Wine*.

Why?

If I tell you because it felt right, that's not enough of an answer. But if I tell you that it seems like this long story—or this series of connected short stories—is all about aging, maybe it'll make more sense.

I was a mature man when I put together this project. I figured—wrongly, as it turned out—that I was halfway through my life. I felt like if I carefully looked back, I might be able to more clearly look forward. "Yesterday's Wine" is a moment when I look back.

The other day I was looking at that famous painting *Nighthawks* by Edward Hopper. It's 1942. We're gazing into the window of a diner. A man and woman sit next to each other on stools. A third sits apart. His back is to us. We don't know anything about these people. But we feel loneliness in the air. We're drawn into a story that isn't being told. So, we make up the story. We fill in the blanks.

That's what I hope folks do when they hear "Yesterday's Wine." Make the story their own.

ME AND PAUL

It's been rough and rocky traveling
But I'm finally standing upright on the ground
After taking several readings
I'm surprised to find my mind's still fairly
  sound

I guess Nashville was the roughest
But I know I've said the same about them all
We received our education
In the cities of the nation, me and Paul

Almost busted in Laredo
But for reasons that I'd rather not disclose
But if you're staying in a motel there and leave
Just don't leave nothing in your clothes

And at the airport in Milwaukee
They refused to let us board the plane at all
They said we looked suspicious
But I believe they like to pick on me and Paul

On a package show in Buffalo
With us and Kitty Wells and Charley Pride
The show was long and we're just sitting there
And we'd come to play and not just for the ride

Well, we drank a lot of whiskey
So I don't know if we went on that night at all
But I don't think they even missed us
I guess Buffalo ain't geared for me and Paul

It was the mid-fifties when one Imperfect Man met another Imperfect Man in Fort Worth, Texas.

Imperfect Man #1—Paul English, Fort Worth native and notorious figure famous for living large outside the law.

Imperfect Man #2—me, a deejay on KCNC, 720 on your dial, spinning and playing live music.

Paul dropped by the studio to see his brother Oliver, a brilliant guitarist who was in my band. I needed a drummer. Paul grabbed a cardboard box and started drumming on it.

Next thing I know, sixty-five years fly by and Paul was still my drummer. Paul was my best friend. Paul was also my security, my bookkeeper, my steady wingman through all the heady storms of life.

Paul's loyalty never wavered—not once. He turned himself into a larger-than-life character, the devil in a black cape with a blood-red lining. But the devil had a heart of gold.

In writing this story about the wandering ways of imperfect men, I thought I could encapsulate our brotherhood in a song. But "Me and Paul" couldn't be contained in a four-minute song. I turned the tune into a full-length book that carried the same name. I wouldn't be surprised if the book becomes a movie.

One thing is certain: I never could have made it without Paul by my side.

I'll never stop singing his song and extolling the blessings that come with true friendship.

GOIN' HOME

The closer I get to my home, Lord, the more I want to be there
There'll be a gathering of loved ones and friends and you know I want to be there
There'll be a mixture of teardrops and flowers, crying and talking for hours
'Bout how wild that I was and if I'd listened to them I wouldn't be there

Well there's old Charlie Toll, they threw away the mold when they made him
And Jimmy McCline it looks like the wine's finally laid him
And Billie McRae that I could beat any day in a card game
And Bessie McNeal but her tears are real, I can see pain

Lord, thanks for the ride I got a feeling inside that I know you
And if you see your way, you're welcome to stay 'cause I'm gonna need you
There's a mixture of teardrops and flowers, crying and talking for hours
About how wild that I was and if I'd listened to them I wouldn't be there

I'd been fooling around with endings and beginnings, mixing up elements from my make-believe life and my real life to where even I didn't know where one stopped and the other started. So before *Yesterday's Wine* started turning sour, I figured I needed a grand conclusion.

I killed off Imperfect Man. I figured that he'd served his purpose by letting me wrap this story around his comings and goings. He'd been a good trooper and deserved a fitting farewell. He'd been so good, in fact, that I decided to give him a treat. I'd let him attend his own funeral.

I suppose lots of us have fooled with that fantasy. Standing over your own grave, getting to hear what friends and family have to say about you. Some are sincerely moved while others are silently snickering. But how do you, Imperfect Man, think about it? What does it feel like to be sitting on the other side of time?

Feels like I'm there and I'm not there. Feels like I'm floating on a cloud, looking down on a world where I was once wondering what it would be like to step out of the picture and reframe everything I once saw. Feels like a song that says hello to everyone I knew even as I say goodbye. A song about going home to a place of tranquility high up in a starlit sky.

What does it feel like to be sitting on the other side of time?

The TRUE ME

I've heard a psychologist say that it isn't healthy for humans to become objects of adoration. Supposedly it corrodes the soul. Well, if that's the case I'm a sick motherfucker with a corroded soul. I love it. I love a crowd. And I love it when a crowd loves me. I don't know a musician or artist—hell, even a plumber—who doesn't want to be adored. It's a form of appreciation for hard work, a soul-to-soul connection that fires me up and makes me want to perform. After eighty years of playing for people, I relish it with the same gusto I had as a kid. Maybe more, because now I know that singing is the best thing I can do to keep my lungs healthy. So now I get to work out even as I entertain fans hungry to have fun and leave their worries at home.

The public creative energy—to perform—is linked to the private creative energy—to write. One feeds the other. In looking back, I see that certain songs give a good glimpse of who I was—and am—in my life journey.

I don't mind revealing the True Me. But as you'll see, today's True Me is a different me from tomorrow's.

SHOTGUN WILLIE

Shotgun Willie sits around in his underwear
Biting on a bullet and pulling out all of
    his hair
Shotgun Willie's got all his family there

Well, you can't make a record if you ain't got
    nothing to say
You can't make a record if you ain't got
    nothing to say
You can't play music if you don't know
    nothing to play

Now John T. Floore was working for the
    Ku Klux Klan
The six-foot-five John T. was a hell
    of a man
Made a lotta money selling sheets on the
    family plan

Shotgun Willie sits around in his underwear
Biting on a bullet and pulling out all
    of his hair
Shotgun Willie's got all his family there

Call it stream of consciousness. Call it slice of life. I just call it saying what's on my mind.

I was in midtown Manhattan, getting ready to record for Atlantic Records. Had never worked in a New York studio before. Because of Jerry Wexler, one of the label's owners who became my lifelong pal, I finally had free rein to use my own musicians and sing whatever I wanted. What I wanted was a new crop of songs. My present situation was happy. After a long, long absence, I had my sister Bobbie back in the band. As kids, the first music we heard and played was gospel music. So we renewed those memories and cut a gospel album, *The Troublemaker*. Jerry was pleased, but now he wanted something more, something new.

Because something new didn't come to mind, I just looked in the mirror and wrote about what I saw: me in my underwear.

When some people write, they immediately judge what they've written. Not me. I could have said to myself, "Who cares about you sitting around in your underwear?" But I didn't. I figured it was a funny image, and besides, it put me in a reflective mood. Got me to thinking about the time I was living in Ridgetop, Tennessee, and my daughter Lana's husband beat her up. So I went over there to beat him up. When he was driving off, I shot his tires out. The cops came and asked, "What's this about you shooting his tires out?" I answered, "Don't know anything about it. He must have run over some of my bullets." That's how Shotgun Willie came to life.

John T. Floore owned a honky-tonk in San Antone and really did sell sheets to the Klan. For no apparent reason, I put him in the song.

"Not sure the song makes sense," I told Wexler.

"Doesn't have to," he said. "It feels great. It feels just like you."

Lana, Billy, and Susie, my three oldest kids, with my first wife Martha.

COUNTRY WILLIE

You called me Country Willie the night you
    walked away
With the one who promised you a life of joy
You thought my life too simple and yours was
    much too gay
To spend it living with a country boy

I'm writing you this letter, I write you every
    day
I hope that you've received the ones before
But I've heard not one word from you and
    every day I pray
That you will not forget your country boy

While you're living in the city with riches
    round your door
Is this your love, is this your kind of joy?
Or do you find there's something missing, does
    your heart cry out for more
And do you sometimes miss your country boy?

A cottage in the country with roses round the
    door
Could not compete with flashing city lights
But it's all I have to offer except for one thing
    more
A heart so filled with love that it could die

Well it's time to end this letter, the light of
    dawn is near
A lonely night has passed but there'll be more
Just one more thing in closing for all the world
    to hear
Come home, I love you
Signed, your country boy

"Hey, Willie, have you ever written an epistolary song?"

"I don't even know how to spell 'epistolary.' What does it mean?"

"A song in the form of a letter."

I had to think back.

"Oh yeah," I said. "I wrote one and signed it 'Country Willie.'"

"Was it true to life?"

"No. I just made it up."

"Why'd you call it 'Country Willie'?"

"I've never liked how some folks look down on the word 'country,'" I said. "I'm as country as corn. Country as cotton. Been a member of the Future Farmers of America ever since I was a kid."

"So your song's about country pride?"

"No. I'm just using this character, this Country Willie, to write a letter begging his sweetie to leave her big-city ways and come home to his loving country arms."

"What was your sweetie's name?"

"I told you," I said. "It's pure fiction."

"But Country Willie is real."

"In the song he is," I said, "but in real life I never stayed up all night writing a letter to anyone. If I'm going to stay up all night, it's to do one thing and one thing only."

"And what is that one thing?"

"Play poker."

DON'T TELL NOAH

Don't tell Noah about the flood
And don't tell Jesus about the blood
And don't tell me that I've lost my mind
'Cause I been crazy all the time

Don't tell the singer you like his song
Then tell him you think he's playin'
    it wrong
Don't tell me that I've lost my mind
'Cause I been crazy all the time

Don't quit trying to change the
    government
And make them see how wrong
    they went
Don't say I ain't got a weird mind
'Cause I been crazy all the time

Don't tell me I told you wrong
It goes like this 'cause I wrote the song
We're wasting time no matter what
    we say
You gotta lead or follow or get outta
    the way

Don't tell Noah
Don't tell Jesus
Don't tell the singer
Don't tell the guitar player

Don't tell Noah about the flood
And don't tell Jesus about the blood
Don't tell me that I've lost my mind
'Cause I been crazy all the time

Preaching is a funny business.

Some preachers like to outright tell people what to think. Others use sermons to make people think. When I was teaching Sunday school, I discovered more questions than answers. The students taught me more than I taught them.

I do believe in saying what I think is wrong. I'm not one to hold my tongue. But over the years, I've come to see that a little reverse psychology can go a long way.

In the guise of a crazy man, I feel freer to speak my mind. And as a crazy man, if I tell you, "Don't do this and don't do that," maybe you'll do just the opposite. Maybe I'll set up a dialogue between you and me. Maybe I'll get you interested in my crazy ideas.

Those ideas might concern questioning authority. I think that's a good thing. Doesn't mean that the authority might not eventually be right. But it does mean that the authority shouldn't be taken at face value.

Everything requires scrutiny. Without scrutiny, we're like sheep being led to the slaughter. With scrutiny, we got a chance of learning the difference between beauty and bullshit.

40,000 folks showed up for a good time at our July 4th Picnic in 1974.

WHO'LL BUY MY MEMORIES

A past that's sprinkled with the blues
A few old dreams that I can't use
Who'll buy my memories of things
    that used to be

There were the smiles before the tears
And with the smiles some better years
Who'll buy my memories of things
    that used to be

When I remember how things were
My memories all lead to her
I'd like to start life anew
But memories just make me blue

A cottage small just built for two
A garden wall with violets blue
Who'll buy my memories of things
    that used to be

Chipping in to feed my granddaughter Rachel while Lana signs my cast.

A songwriter is also a salesman. At least I am.

Early in my life, when I was selling vacuum cleaners and encyclopedias door-to-door, I sometimes had a guilty conscience. I didn't like talking folks into buying things they didn't need, especially young couples who looked like they were barely able to pay the rent.

When it came to selling music, I never had that attitude. I've always believed in the sincerity of my songs.

The selling process is twofold: As a writer, I have to compose a song with a message that connects; and as a singer, I have to sell my song onstage. I want the listener to say, "Man, I can buy into Willie's story. I know he's coming from the heart."

This song got some play in the nineties when the IRS was on my ass and I needed money. To placate the Feds, I said I'd make an album and give them the proceeds. I called it *The IRS Tapes: Who'll Buy My Memories?* I kept production costs down by singing solo, just me and my trusty Trigger. Sales were good and the tax issue was eventually resolved.

One critic accused me of selling out. That made me laugh. "Selling out" is a term that warms my heart, especially when a promoter tells me my show has "sold out" or a record store says they've "sold out" of my album.

I've been trying to sell out all my life.

TOUCH ME

Touch me
Touch the hand of a man who once owned all the world

Touch me
Touch the arms that once held all the charms of the world's sweetest girl

Touch me
Maybe someday you may need to know how it feels when you lose

So touch me
And you'll know how you'd feel with the blues

Watch me
Watch the eyes that have seen all the heartbreak and pain in the land

And be thankful
That you're happy though standing so close to the world's bluest man

Don't forget me
Take a good look at someone who's lost everything he can lose

Then touch me
And you'll know how you'd feel with the blues

This was written when I was in my twenties.

I'd gotten a recording contract from Liberty Records. That was a big deal for Country Willie. Liberty was the home of Julie London, a super-sexy jazz singer who hit big with "Cry Me a River." Vikki Carr was also on Liberty, along with the Chipmunks, a high-pitched novelty act selling millions of records. Liberty might have viewed me as a novelty, but I didn't care. This was my first contract with a national label.

I initially sang "Touch Me" in Nashville with strings, background singers, and no less than four guitarists. I had no complaints. But my producer, Joe Allison, thought I could do it better, so he flew me out to LA for a second session, an even more elaborate affair. (I later learned that two of the studio musicians were Leon Russell on piano and Glen Campbell on guitar.) Allison still wasn't happy, because the background singers couldn't follow my phrasing. They complained about my peculiar sense of time. They were right to complain.

At the same time, in 1961 I was too dumb to care about the complaints. I couldn't sing any other way. When we went back to Nashville for a third session, the results—at least to my ears—weren't much different. Can't remember which vocal version Allison decided to release. It didn't matter, because "Touch Me" didn't touch too many listeners. Hearing it today, though, brings a smile to my face. My songs are my babies, and though the birthing process wasn't easy, "Touch Me" survived. Couldn't ask for more.

My good buddy, Leon Russell.

FACE OF A FIGHTER

These lines in my face caused from worry
Grow deeper as you walk out of sight
Mine is the face of a fighter
But my heart has just lost the fight

Round one, you told me you loved me
And I felt my heart falling there and then
The last round, you walked tall and left me
And I guess my heart's losing again

Mine is the face of a fighter
I fought for your love with all my might
Mine is the face of a fighter
But my heart has just lost the fight

This song came to me ages ago when I hardly had any lines on my face. I hardly had the face of a fighter. I had the face of a scrappy young man. In these lyrics, I guess I was projecting ahead.

Today I've got all the creases, lines, and wrinkles of a man who has turned ninety. Today I have the face of someone who's been fighting the good fight forever.

Makeup artists often ask me when I'm about to be interviewed on TV, "Is it okay if I touch up your face, Mr. Nelson?"

"I'm afraid not," I always answer. "It's hopeless."

"Oh, I think I can smooth things out."

"I'm sure you can, but at this point I feel like I've earned every line and wrinkle. I'll just go on as is."

And I do. It's one of the great pleasures of old age. Accepting who you are, body and soul.

When we're young, we don't want to look beat-up. Vanity tells us to hide the face of the fighter. Vanity says, "Put on a good face." But in time, vanity gives way to common sense. And common sense says, "Who cares?"

Today I have the face of someone who's been fighting the good fight forever.

IT GETS EASIER

It gets easier as we get older
It gets easier to say "not today"
And it gets easier as we get older
To say "go away and not today"

I don't have to do
One damn thing
That I don't want to do
Except for missing you
And that won't go away

It gets easier to say "some other time"
It gets easier to tell the world to wait
And it gets easier to watch the world
 fly by
And tell it "I will catch up, but not
 today"

"It Gets Easier" is age appropriate. I wrote it only five or six years ago. It says what I couldn't say in "Face of a Fighter" because, in my twenties, I really didn't know what was heading my way.

I'm as happy now as I've ever been. And one of the reasons is because I can say "not today." As a youngster, I thought that if I didn't grab it, I'd lose it. I was driven by a force that I couldn't name but I could sure feel. I was driven to grab success. Well, success is elusive. Success means many different things. I thought it had something to do with hit records. I was wrong. It has everything to do with accepting yourself. Accepting your limitations as well as your strengths. Accepting the certainty that you're not going to please everyone.

Yet even in this song about self-acceptance, there's a troubling thought about something that isn't easy: It isn't easy missing you.

I ask myself the question, "Who is 'you'?"

And the only answer is, "I don't know."

I'll just have to keep writing and singing to find out.

Performing at the Armadillo in Austin, Texas, back in my younger and shorter-haired days, with Mickey Raphael on the harmonica, Jackie Deaton on bass, and Jimmy Day on pedal steel guitar.

TRUE LOVE

I followed you to hell and back
I'll follow you again
No matter where you take me
It's someplace that I ain't been
And I'll go to hell believing
True love, you're still my friend

From the start to the finish
And until the bitter end
I'll live my life believing
True love, you're still my friend

When the whole damn thing is over
And we reach our journey's end
I'll leave this world believing
True love, you're still my friend

The road was always rocky
Trouble waiting around every bend
I'll go to hell believing
True love, you're still my friend

You taught me how to twist
  and turn
And bend before I break
And fake it till I make it
All for true love's sake

You're worth all the heartaches
And I'd do it all again
I'll leave this world believing
True love, you're still my friend

I can't escape this prison
This cell I'm living in
Where memories guard the inmates
And true love, you're still my friend

In drawing a self-portrait, it wouldn't bother me to paint all the lines and wrinkles on my well-worn fighting face. But I'd add a certain look in my eyes—an intense gaze—that would reveal a central fact about me: I'm damn stubborn. That stare would say, "I do believe in one thing so strongly that, come hell or high water, I'll never change my mind." That one thing is True Love.

I met True Love when I was a kid. My grandparents were all about it. Sister Bobbie was all about it. I chased it and thought I caught it, only to watch it run away. I chased it some more, caught it again, and then, when everything seemed to be going right, I found a way to mess it up. The love was true, but I wasn't.

I didn't give up on True Love, or you could say True Love didn't give up on me. Either way, I kept it in sight. I believed in its righteousness. Apart from the True Love of spiritual light, I knew there was the True Love of romance. Finding that True Love was worth all the effort.

I came to learn that True Love lived in two places at once. It lived right here in my heart; it was my heart's desire. But it also lived outside me. It lived in the sky where eagles fly. It lived in the ocean where dolphins swim. It was everywhere.

True Love kept me high, kept me afloat, kept me from falling into cynicism or despair.

The singer says he can't escape the jail where memories guard the door. But the man who wrote the song says that True Love has set him free.

I DON'T GO TO FUNERALS

I don't go to funerals
And I won't be at mine
I'll be somewhere looking back
At loved ones left behind

My life has been a wonder
I found my place in time
But I don't go to funerals
And I won't be at mine

I'll be somewhere singing songs
With all those dear old friends of mine
Life is great but I can't wait
To make our memories rhyme

Those who've gone before me
Will save my place in line
I don't go to funerals
And I won't be at mine

There'll be a big ol' picking party
When it comes my time
Me and Waylon, John and Kris
And our sweetheart Patsy Cline

Merle and Grady and Freddy Powers
And all those pals of mine
But I don't go to funerals
And I won't be at mine

Somewhere I hear angel voices
Singing in the wind
Saying how it won't be long
Till it's time to fly again

Life is sweet and love is good
And we have had a good time
But I don't go to funerals
And I sure won't be at mine

Kris Kristofferson talking to clean-cut versions of me and Waylon.

I'd never compare myself to Walt Whitman. I'm a pretty good songwriter. He was a genius, some say the greatest poet in American history. When he wrote *Leaves of Grass* in the middle of the nineteenth century, his free verse was considered radical. He didn't bother to rhyme because, well, who said poems gotta rhyme? In "Song of Myself," a section of *Leaves of Grass*, he wrote, "Do I contradict myself? / Very well then I contradict myself / (I am large, I contain multitudes.)"

Here's one of my big contradictions: Fifty years before I wrote "I Don't Go to Funerals," I wrote "Goin' Home," the finale to *Yesterday's Wine*. That's where I had Imperfect Man attend his own funeral. In old age, I flip the script and say the opposite. Rather than wanting to hear what's happening at my burial, I'd rather be off singing songs with my pals in the Great Beyond. Funerals are flat-out depressing. I avoid them. And I'm avoiding mine.

It's not that I'm afraid to deal with death. Like lots of my recent songs, "I Don't Go to Funerals" faces the issue of mortality. I'm not morbid about mortality. I can even look forward to reuniting with spirits that have gone on before me. I work hard to keep my body healthy while, at the same time, I can see how leaving my body might be a relief.

WRITE YOUR OWN SONGS

You call us heathens with zero respect for the
  law
We are only songwriters just writing our songs
  and that's all
We write what we live and we live what we
  write, is that wrong?

If you think it is, Mr. Music Executive
Why don't you write your own songs

And don't listen to mine, they might run you
  crazy
They might make you dwell on your feelings a
  moment too long
We're making you rich and you're already lazy

So just lay on your ass and get richer
Or write your own songs

Mr. Purified Country, don't you know what the
  whole thing's about
Is your head up your ass so far that you can't
  pull it out
The world's getting smaller and everyone in it
  belongs

And if you can't see that, Mr. Purified Country
Why don't you just write your own songs

Waylon and me decidedly less clean cut.

I get pissed off plenty. And no portrait of the True Me would be complete without showing my angry side. If you go through life without getting furious at someone or something, you're hardly human. It's just a matter of how and when you release the emotion.

Writing "Write Your Own Songs" was a big release. In 1982, I sang it with Waylon Jennings on *WWII*, the second album we did as a duo.

Waylon was the perfect partner. He was a force of nature, and his nature, though loving, was also filled with fury. He suffered no fools and, like me, had run into any number of fools who found themselves in charge of record companies.

It's more my style to praise the good guys, execs like Jerry Wexler and producers like Daniel Lanois, who helped me in countless ways. But the jerks who thought they understood my music better than me needed to be memorialized. And a song seemed like the right vehicle.

After the tune was released, some fans wanted to know whether I was referring to specific people. In each case, I denied it. My denials weren't entirely truthful. I could have called out these guys, but what would be the point? They knew who they were.

I imagined them listening to the song. I imagined them squirming. I imagined that I gave them reason to question themselves. But I also knew that my imagination was faulty. Chances are, the execs I was targeting never even heard the damn thing.

LAWS OF NATURE

I get my energy from the sun
And I'm not the only one
I feel better when I'm done
I get my energy from the sun

I get my oxygen from the air
There's plenty for me and plenty to spare
And I can find it anywhere
I get my oxygen from the air

I plant my seeds in the howling gale
But the laws of nature still prevail
Look at them seeds and look at me
The apple didn't fall far from the tree

I get my water from the rain
If it don't rain I'll die
Stormy weather saves my life
Sometimes I laugh and wonder why

In calling this chapter "The True Me," I realized that without my sister Bobbie I'd be a completely different me. By modeling what it means to be a fine musician, she pointed me in the right direction. By modeling what it means to be a loving human being, she taught me the meaning of kindness. I wish I could be as forgiving as she was. I wish I could have her compassion.

When she passed at age ninety, I went back to listen to some of the songs we played together. Many were the hymns of our childhood. Others, like "Laws of Nature," were written when she was close by. Bobbie was someone who accepted whatever came her way. She did so with gratitude.

Thinking of her wisdom, I began to understand how without storms—whether the rainstorms of nature or the emotional storms of life—we couldn't survive. Intuitively, that's something Bobbie understood.

She endured hardships that would destroy most people. Her ability to do so rested in her understanding that storms are transitory. She understood that the laws of nature are based on abundance and regeneration. Like love, nature's energy is infinite.

Bobbie's beautiful spirit informs this song. As I sang it, the sweetness of her piano calmed and comforted me. I knew I could never have gotten this far without her. Bobbie anchored my restless soul.

LONELY PLACES

The feeling was there when I was a little kid and put together a little book of lyrics. The sentiments were rife with loneliness. The song titles tell the story. "Faded Love and Wasted Dream." "I Guess I Was Born to Be Blue." "I'll Wander Alone."

You might cite its source as the death of my grandfather four years earlier, but I don't see that as the cause. I think I was simply emulating songs I was listening to on the radio. Jimmie Rodgers, who died the year I was born, 1933, sang songs like "Train Whistle Blues," "Jimmie's Texas Blues," "That's Why I'm Blue," "Those Gambler's Blues." Jimmie Rodgers, the Singing Brakeman, was always singing the blues. In 1943, when I was ten, I heard Big Bill Broonzy singing "See See Rider." The feeling of the blues, whether sung by Blacks or whites, men or women, got into me. I was lucky because, I'd later learn, the blues is the foundation of American music. The blues is the foundation of the human condition.

The blues comes from a lonely place. And though I've been surrounded by wonderful people throughout my life, that lonely place never disappeared. I could sense it. I could tap into it when I wrote. Even if the loneliness never abated, singing about it helped relieve that sinking feeling that life, for all its joy, is often a sad, sad affair.

STAY AWAY FROM LONELY PLACES

Stay away from lonely places
Just follow the crowd
And stay around familiar faces
And play the music loud

Be seen at all the parties
And dress yourself in style
Stay away from lonely places
For a while

Stay away from lonely places
Till you learn to live alone
Someone's outstretched arms are
    waiting
To stay with you at least till dawn

And remember that sorrow prospers
In a heart that never smiles
So stay away from lonely places
For a while

True blues give me solace. They're timeless. It's comforting to know that some musical forms are here to stay. Their staying power emanates from the honesty of their message and the simplicity of their expression.

In this old blues ditty, I extend a warning to avoid what I know can never be avoided: those nights when, in the midnight hour, you're alone and filled with despair. My advice is to find a diversion. Find a party. Find a friend. Do anything but give in to the depression that hangs over you like a dark cloud.

Depression has a mind all its own. It also has a purpose all its own: to take you out.

They have pills for depression and God knows I'm not against modern medicine. They have therapists to treat depression and I'm all for therapists.

But as a singer dispensing a modest dose of wisdom, I'm just saying it's good to avoid depressing places.

I believe that my advice is sound. But in dispensing it, I know it's futile.

The blues—despite the best diversions, pills, and therapists in the land—are here to stay.

The blues is
the foundation
of the human
condition.

I'M STILL NOT OVER YOU

Today I made a point to go somewhere I
    knew you'd be
I had to know if you still had the same effect
    on me
And the moment that I saw you there I knew
No matter what I do I'm still not over you

I'm still not over you
That feeling's still the same
And I'm still not over you,
I find that nothing's changed

And perhaps someday
I'll find somebody new
But now it's much too soon
I'm still not over you

I can't explain why seeing you affects my
    sanity
But when I see you I become strange and
    differently
And the moment that I saw you there I knew
No matter what I do I'm still not over you

Playing bass with Ray Price and the Cherokee Cowboys.

I love making albums dedicated to the memories of my mentors. I had no better mentor than Ray Price. When he died in 2013, my heart was broken. Ray had shown up during dark days and brought light into my life.

Every time he sang "Night Life," I broke into a smile. When he asked me to join his famous Cherokee Cowboys in 1961, I really wasn't qualified to be a bass player. But Ray believed in me more than I believed in myself.

In 2007, Merle Haggard and I went on the road with Ray, then eighty-one. We called it the Last of the Breed Tour. After our final date, Merle told me, "That old man gave us singing lessons. He just sang so good. He sat there with the mic to his mouth and got right to the middle of every note. And you and me, Willie, we're still trying to find the middle. Well, Ray found it."

In 2016, I released *For the Good Times: A Tribute to Ray Price*, recorded in the same studio where Ray sang his final album, *Beauty Is . . . The Final Sessions*. I included "I'm Still Not Over You," a song I wrote in the sixties, the same decade when Ray and I became running buddies, because it expressed exactly how I felt.

I'll never stop missing the man.

"That old man gave us singing lessons."

WAKE ME WHEN IT'S OVER

I'm getting tired now, I gotta get some
    sleep now
Guess I've been worried much too long
And don't wake me till it's over
And the need for you is gone

I was so happy before I loved you
I wanna be like I was before
And don't wake me till it's over
When I won't want you anymore

My eyes are getting weak now, I gotta
    get some sleep now
I gotta rest my aching head
I just wanna lay here, just let me stay
    here
Till the blues get up and leave my bed

Good night, darling, good night
    darling
Good night forevermore
And don't wake me till it's over
When I won't love you anymore

Oklahoma's been good to me. Hell, all the states have been good to me, but especially those that I could count on in the fifties when I was struggling to stay afloat.

I was playing a barroom in Durant, just over the border north of Denison, Texas. Denison was dry but you could drink in Durant. Unsavory beer joints called "buckets of blood" were busy enough to hire a band.

I got through playing the last set. The crowd was rowdy and ready for more, but I was exhausted. I was halfway out the door when a fellow came up and said, "Hey, Willie, I got five bucks to spare if you sing me a song that keeps me from killing the lady I love."

His request stopped me cold. He was my age, twenty-five or so. In his beat-up brown cowboy hat and muddy boots, he looked lost. And desperate.

"Just sleep it off," I suggested.

"I need a song," he insisted. "I need one of those songs that makes everything wrong seem right."

Weirdly enough, I'd just written something that I hoped might fit the bill. That was the first time I sang a live version of "Wake Me When It's Over."

"That's all I needed to hear," said the troubled soul. "Now I can go home and go to sleep."

"I hope it's over when you wake."

"It won't be," he said. "It never is."

Touring is never without its hazards. After our tour bus "Pauletta" broke down in west Texas, me and Paul decided to hang out on the roof.

ANGEL FLYING TOO CLOSE TO THE GROUND

If you had not have fallen
Then I would not have found you
Angel flying too close to the ground

And I patched up your broken wing
And hung around awhile
Trying to keep your spirits up
And your fever down

I knew someday that you would fly away
For love's the greatest healer to be found
So leave me if you need to, I will still remember
Angel flying too close to the ground

Fly on, fly on past the speed of sound
I'd rather see you up than see you down
So leave me if you need to, I will still remember
My angel flying too close to the ground

During those times when I was doing heavy reading and seeking unanswerable questions, I stumbled on this quote: "Knowledge is life with wings."

When I thought of wings, I thought of angels. I thought of angels flying around with a knowledge that could ease our troubled minds.

I had known angelic women. Their sweetness felt heavenly. Their purpose appeared only to love unselfishly. I imagined one such angel entering the life of a difficult man. To be with him required that, rather than soar, she descend. If she wants to live on his level, she must fall.

Determined to repair the damage, he does so sadly, knowing that this angel is more than he deserves. Her fate is elsewhere. Her flight, her departure, is inevitable.

I've been singing this sorrowful song since I wrote it in the eighties. I can't tell you how many people have asked me to name the angel I have in mind. My answer is always the same:

"It could be any one of a thousand angels. You name her. You tell me who she is."

"Knowledge
is life
with wings."

MAN WITH THE BLUES

If you need some advice in being lonely
If you need a little help in feeling blue
If you need some advice on how to cry all night
Come to me, I'm the man with the blues

I'm the man with a hundred thousand heartaches
I've got a good selection old and new
So if you need a little shove in fouling up in love
Come to me, I'm the man with the blues

I wrote this song over sixty years ago. I was somewhere in Waxahachie, Texas, hanging out in the basement of a friend. We were drinking some beers when he started asking me advice about his love life. I don't know where he got the idea that I knew anything about love. I was in my early twenties and doing my best—or my worst—to mess up my marriage.

"You've got all this confidence, Willie," he said. "You're a man who knows what he's doing."

"I'm more like a man with the blues."

I liked the way that line sounded, so I picked up my guitar and the story came to life.

Decades later, I became friends with B.B. King, a real bluesman. We started talking about what it means to have the blues.

"If you're breathing," said B.B., "you got the blues."

"Even if you're happy?" I asked.

"Especially if you're happy," he answered. "You live long enough and learn that happiness is a sometime thing. Happiness comes and goes. But the blues is something we're born with. The blues lives in your bones."

PERMANENTLY LONELY

Don't be concerned, it's time I learned
That those who play with fire get burned
But I'll be all right in a little while
But you'll be permanently lonely

Don't be too quick to pity me
Don't salve my heart with sympathy
'Cause I'll be all right in a little while
But you'll be permanently lonely

The world looks on with wonder
And pity at your kind
'Cause it knows that the future
Is not very pretty for your kind

Your kind will always be running
And wondering what's happened to hearts
That you've broken and left all alone
But we'll be all right in a little while

But you'll be permanently lonely

Running . . . lonely . . .

I liked this song well enough to record it at least five different times. I've probably performed it live five hundred times.

First it was released on *Live Country Music Concert* from Panther Hall in Fort Worth, in 1966. Two years later, it came out on an RCA album, *Good Times*. Then, in 1981, producer Chips Moman had me sing it on the *Always on My Mind* album. And to prove it was always on my mind, I did it twice again: in 1992 on *The IRS Tapes: Who'll Buy My Memories?* and in 2014 with sister Bobbie on *December Day*.

Why should I have such a lifelong fascination with a song? Maybe because I allowed myself to make up a story that was worlds away from my true feelings about women. I've never scorned women or cast them as villains. But in "Permanently Lonely," I'm able to create a character whose anger at the opposite sex is so intense that he wishes his lady permanent misery. I've known guys like that. I've felt the full force of their fury. And even though I've never shared their bitterness, I realized that in the tales they told was high drama.

High drama makes for good stories. Tortured passion makes for good songs. And the man whose life has led him to say "I'll be fine, but you'll never know anything but heartache" needs to sing about it because, in feeling that way, he sure as hell isn't alone.

IT SHOULD BE EASIER NOW

Now that I've made up my mind you're gone
It should be easier now
Perhaps now my heart will stop hanging on
It should be easier now

The lesson I learned from you gold can't buy
A heart can be broken and still survive
Thanks to you now a much wiser man am I
And it should be easier now

The worst now is over, I've stood the test
It should be easier now
They say everything happens for the best
And it should be easier now

The wounds in my heart you carved deep and
   wide
Hollowed and washed with the tears that I've
   cried
But now there'll be more room for love inside
And it should be easier now

I'm presenting myself to
the world the only way
I know how: plainly.

A clean-shaven man with a conservative haircut is wearing a black turtleneck sweater and neatly pressed brown slacks. He has just turned thirty. Standing before a wall of flagstaff stone, he holds a microphone in his right hand. To his left are four female singers, each identically coiffed in equally conservative hairdos, each wearing identical green blazers. Every time the man sings, "It should be easier now," they sing the same words after him.

The man is virtually expressionless. As he vocalizes, he moves his head only slightly. He doesn't permit himself to smile until the song is over. And even that smile is fleeting. You'd hardly call him charismatic. If he makes an impression, it's far from memorable. You might not even realize that the man is me.

It's the sixties and I'm appearing on TV. I have no image to speak of, no Stetson cowboy hat or fancy boots, no sparkly outfit. I'm presenting myself to the world the only way I know how: plainly.

I'm plainly content to just stand there and sing. The girls next to me are far from sexy. They're girls from next door. I'm the guy from next door.

I've got this one little song that says I've been hurt but not enough to do me in. I look like a man who can survive the slings and arrows of outrageous fortune.

I look pretty steady. I have no idea what lies ahead. But I know that this song, as modest as it is, is making things easier for me. Songs always do.

RAINY DAY BLUES

Well it's cloudy in the morning gonna be
    raining in the afternoon
Cloudy in the morning and it's gonna be
    raining in the afternoon
If you don't like this rainy weather you
    better pack your bags and move

But if you're running from it, brother,
    the only road that I can see
If you're running from it, brother, the
    only road that I can see
Is the road that leads to nowhere and
    nowhere is a fool like me

Rain keep a falling, falling round my
    windowpane
Rain keep a falling, falling round my
    windowpane
Ain't never seen so much rainy weather,
    guess I'll never see the sun again

Save your dimes and nickels, save 'em
    for a rainy day
Save your dimes and nickels, save 'em
    for a rainy day
It ain't gonna keep the rain from coming
    but at least you know you've paid
    your way

With Wynton Marsalis.

The bridge that will never burn down is the one built by the blues.

The blues are too deep, too true, too universal, too present to ever be lost to the past.

I wrote this traditional twelve-bar blues thinking of all the twelve-bar blues I heard as a kid. I love the pattern because it's so basic:

The first two lines are identical, and the third line rhymes with the first two.

These are the blues played by a long line of Texans like Lightnin' Hopkins and Stevie Ray Vaughan, Mississippians like Robert Johnson and Muddy Waters, ladies like Big Mama Thornton and Etta James.

I once asked Ray Charles, who was born in rural Georgia in 1930, only three years before me, when he first heard the blues.

"Can't remember *not* hearing the blues," he said. "Even when Mama took me to our little church, it sounded like preacher was singing the blues. 'Is that the blues?' I asked Mama. 'The good news blues,' she said."

Ray confirmed what I already felt: the bluest blues are good.

I wrote "Rainy Day Blues" in 1960. The label on the record read, "Paul Buskirk and His Little Men featuring Hugh Nelson." Hugh's my middle name. I wasn't happy that I didn't get full credit. Nearly fifty years later I couldn't be happier when I got to sing that same blues with trumpeter Wynton Marsalis at Jazz at Lincoln Center.

B.B. King said it best: "The blues are all around me, and I wouldn't want it any other way."

THERE ARE WORSE THINGS THAN BEING ALONE

We finally said all our final goodbyes
And tear after tear fell from everyone's eyes
But just like a funeral where nobody dies
There's worse things than being alone

There are worse things than being alone
Like a full house and nobody home
If the feeling keeps changing then
    something's gone wrong
And there's worse things than being alone

Well past my halfway in time
But I still have a lot on my mind
And there's one thing for certain beyond
    right or wrong
There's worse things than being alone

To end this "Lonely Places" chapter, I'm listening to a song that challenges the nature of loneliness.

My buddy Zeke used to say, "You can be surrounded by a whole posse of pardners and still be the loneliest man in the room."

I asked him what that meant.

"Some folks have a hole in their souls. They're born lonely, live lonely, and die lonely. Then you got cowpokes who can be alone out in the prairie for months at a time and never feel lonely at all."

"Why is that?"

"They like their own company."

Do I like mine? I believe so. I wrote this song when I turned sixty. That's why I sang "past my halfway in time." It seemed like the right time and the right statement. I could be alone with my music. Alone with my thoughts. Even alone with my loneliness.

Jimmy Bowen, the producer, thought well enough of the song to get Jimmy Webb to write a lush string arrangement. When I sang it, though, with a full orchestra, I did feel a little lonely. But then again, someone once said, "When it comes to writing songs, 'Lonely' is Willie's middle name."

Hanging out with Ray Charles and friends.

STILL IS STILL MOVING

To be still or not to be still—that is the question.

It wasn't until my sixties that I learned the answer: You can be both at once. You can be still in your heart and moving in your mind. You can be still in your thoughts and moving in your plans. You can be steady in the moment even as you figure out your next move in the next moment.

I'm always moving, yet I'm always still—still the same combination of action and inaction. I'm as self-reflective as I am proactive. I'm moved by the things that I learn in reflection, and I stay still until I understand how to apply those lessons learned.

It's all instinct. When to stay still. When to move. When to stop. When to start. It's all interconnected in ways that defy analysis. I don't have to figure it out. I don't have to fear it. I just have to do that dance between action and inaction. That dance never stops. It's the movement of life. It's the still movement that makes our journey mysterious and, if we don't worry about it too much, a hell of a lot of fun.

STILL IS STILL MOVING TO ME

Still is still moving to me
I swim like a fish in the sea all the time
But if that's what it takes to be free I don't
    mind
Still is still moving to me

And it's hard to explain how I feel
It won't go in words but I know that it's real
I can be moving or I can be still
But still is still moving to me

My buddy Billy Joe Shaver said that moving is the closest thing to being free. I say the next best thing is being on the bus thinking that you might soon be moving.

"Still Is Still Moving to Me" came out a month before my sixtieth birthday in 1993 on *Across the Borderline.* The title hit me when I was riding bikes with my wife Annie and my boys Micah and Lukas up in Wisconsin. The song had a positive propulsion. When the lyrics came, they were few but felt right. I stated the paradox and just let it hang out there. The music was moving and that was enough.

Don Was produced the album. I also got help from Paul Simon, Bob Dylan, and Kris Kristofferson. Mark Rothbaum, my manager, said it was my first album to show up on the pop charts in eight years. A few days later, Mark said something else: The new exec in charge of Columbia Nashville, my label for the past eighteen years, was kicking me off the roster.

Mark was furious. I wasn't. My sales couldn't compare to superstars like Garth Brooks and Alan Jackson. I accepted that. I also accepted the fact that record companies, though they like describing themselves as "families," are no such thing. They're profit centers. On the other hand, when I decided to call my band Family, I wasn't thinking of money. I was thinking of loyalty and love.

Besides, before being dropped by Columbia, I had already written a mantra that sustained my spirit. "Still Is Still Moving to Me" was the song that let me accept this incident with serenity. I was old enough to know that businessmen come and go. I also knew that I wasn't going to disappear—and neither were my songs.

Me and Paul Simon take the stage.

WHO DO I KNOW
IN DALLAS

Who do I know in Dallas
Who can I call on the phone

Who do I know in Dallas
That will help me forget that I'm alone

Shirley consoled me in Phoenix
And Jeannie in old San Antone

But who do I know in Dallas
That will help me forget that I'm alone

I can't spend the night without someone
The lonelies will drive me insane

So who do I know in Dallas
That will make me be happy I came

I'm not telling you who I knew in Dallas. Even if I did remember, I wouldn't tell you. It would ruin the song.

This is another one of those "Still Is Still Moving to Me" sentiments. I wrote it in my formative years when Texas was the one place I could count on. The Texas barrooms were always good to me.

Before I could afford a bus, I traveled in old station wagons or broken-down vans or whatever vehicle would get me from one town to the next. I often wrote on the fly. My writing partner Hank Cochran, who had missed out on "Hello Walls" when he left the room to take a phone call, was determined not to miss out again.

"You don't mind if I go with you on one of your Texas trips, do you?" he asked.

I loved Hank, so I was happy to have him come along. We had played Amarillo and were headed to Dallas when he said, "Willie, who do you know in Dallas?"

"Lots of folks."

"Well, maybe you should write a song to one of them."

"Great, you gave me the title. Now can you give me the first line?" I asked.

"Something about picking up the phone so you won't be alone."

By the time we reached the outskirts of Dallas, we'd fashioned a melody and, as usual, kept the story simple.

"What do you think?" I asked Hank.

"I still want to know who you know in Dallas."

LONDON

The streets are dark and quiet in
   London after midnight
Listen
The silence is the master of darkness
And London can sleep tonight
Protected by the master

London, London
You scream the largest portion of
   the day

London, London
Rest your lungs, tomorrow's on
   its way

My good buddy Roger Miller wrote "England Swings" in the mid-sixties. He was the first one to tell me how much Londoners liked country music. When I arrived several years later, the scene had exploded. Carnaby Street was a carnival of crazy clothes. Everyone was tripping. London seemed like the center of the universe, and I was happy to be there. Especially happy to find that audiences were receptive.

I was staying in a hippie hotel in Chelsea. It was party central. Noise night and day. I'm not averse to partying and was certainly happy to discover that the English weed was mellow. Maybe it was the mellowness of the weed that had me move in a different direction. Rather than write about the partying, I decided to leave the party and walk by the Thames. It was the middle of the night and, at last, it was quiet. The sky was clear. A crescent moon hung overhead. I loved the silence. I loved the darkness. It occurred to me that "silence is the master of darkness." I liked the line, even though I wasn't sure what it meant. Other lines came to mind. Quiet lines, silent lines. When I got back to the hotel, I spoke rather than sang those lines: "London can sleep tonight protected by the master." With that, I drifted off.

By morning, the silence had surrendered to London's great roar. But I wanted to sing about the silence. I wanted to capture that moment when my heart was still.

DEVIL IN A SLEEPING BAG

We were headed home to Austin
Caught pneumonia on the road
Taking it home to Connie and the kids
A wheel ran off and jumped a railroad
Then ran through a grocery store
If you want to buy a bus I'm taking bids

And the devil shivered in his sleeping bag
He said traveling on the road is such a
   drag
If we can make it home by Friday we can
   brag
And the devil shivered in his sleeping bag

Well, I just got back from New York City
Kris and Rita done it all
Raw perfection there for all the world
   to see
Lord I heard an angel singing in the
   Philharmonic Hall
Rita Coolidge, Rita Coolidge cleft for me

And the devil shivered in his sleeping bag
He said traveling on the road is such a
   drag
If we can make it home by Friday we can
   brag
And the devil shivered in his sleeping bag

Songs are like photographs, moments in time captured in rhyme and wrapped in melody. Even those that don't make complete sense refresh my memory and help me relive events that would otherwise vanish into thin air.

This story is pretty clear—to a point.

It's another "still is still moving" song, a travel ditty that documents a trip taken back to Austin from New York, where I'd heard Kris Kristofferson and his then-wife Rita Coolidge perform beautifully. At the time I was married to Connie Koepke and eager to get home to see her and our darling daughters, Amy and Paula.

Then problems popped up. I caught pneumonia and our trusty ol' bus turned out to be not so trusty. We lost a wheel and ran off the road. All that would be enough to upset the calmest of men. But Paul English never batted an eye. Conked out in a sleeping bag, he remained undisturbed in dreamland.

Paul liked this devil image he cultivated—the cape, the long sideburns, the pointy goatee. And especially the pistols he was always careful to carry. Even though he was doing a lot more snoring than shivering, I liked the idea of a hot-blooded devil unable to keep warm.

"Was I really shivering, Willie?" Paul asked me when I played him the song.

"Poetic license, Paul."

"Poetic license lets you lie?"

"Poetic license will help make you famous."

Paul smiled. That's all he needed to hear.

Paul in full regalia.

ON THE ROAD AGAIN

On the road again
Just can't wait to get on the road again
The life I love is making music with my friends
And I can't wait to get on the road again

On the road again
Going places that I've never been
Seeing things that I may never see again
And I can't wait to get on the road again

On the road again
Like a band of gypsies we go down the
   highway
We're the best of friends
Insisting that the world keep turning our way

And our way
Is on the road again

If someone asked me to write an anthem, I'd freeze. That's way above my pay grade. An anthem is too serious for me. I think of "The Star-Spangled Banner" or "America the Beautiful." And yet . . .

In 1980, I got top billing in a movie, *Honeysuckle Rose*. I had no illusions about my acting chops. Slim Pickens, one of the costars, said it best: "No one plays Willie Nelson better than Willie Nelson."

At one point during the production, I was on a private plane with producer Sydney Pollack and director Jerry Schatzberg.

"The movie needs a song," said Sydney.

"A love song?" I asked.

"It'd be better to write something about being on the road."

Off the cuff, I scribbled down some words and read them out loud: "On the road again . . . can't wait to get on the road again . . ."

Sydney didn't look thrilled. "Where's the melody?" he asked.

"Just around the corner," I said. "It'll be here in no time."

Sydney still wasn't thrilled. A week later, though, when the melody showed up, Sydney was satisfied.

The song got so big that when *Honeysuckle Rose* aired on TV, they retitled the film *On the Road Again*.

Without knowing or trying, in a few little lines I'd written the story of my life.

ONE DAY AT A TIME

I live one day at a time
I dream one dream at a time
Yesterday's dead and tomorrow is blind
And I live one day at a time

I guess that you're surprised to see me back
   at home
But you know how much I miss you when
   I'm gone

Don't ask how long I plan to stay 'cause it
   never crossed my mind
I live one day at a time

See that sparrow fly across the cloudy sky
Searching for a patch of sunlight, so am I
I wish I didn't have to follow and perhaps I
   won't in time
I live one day at a time

Clichés get a bad rap. A good cliché can make for a good song.

Most clichés get to be clichés because they contain an element of truth.

I wrote "One Day at a Time" during my clean-cut Nashville days. When I wrote it, I was having some marital problems—no surprise there—and found that the song took an unexpected turn.

My original idea was to simply say it's important not to get ahead of ourselves. Today is Monday. Don't worry about what happened Sunday or what's going to happen Tuesday. I set out a simple premise.

But often when I write, these simple premises evaporate. Complexity sets in. And suddenly the song turns out to have a story I didn't even know was there.

After being gone for a spell, a man finds himself back home. He sweetly tells his woman how much he missed her. Seems like the song is going to be about a happy reunion. Except it isn't. If she asks how long he plans to stay, he suddenly freezes. Committing to her never even crossed his mind. Who is this cold-hearted bastard?

He's like a bird searching for sunlight, following a fate that he can neither name nor understand.

He may be living one day at a time, but each day is filled with uncertainty. Each day may take him down a path that, whether he likes it or not, he feels forced to follow.

What begins as a simple cliché ends up as a bewildering mystery.

But often when I write, these simple premises evaporate. Complexity sets in.

TEXAS

Listen to my song
And if you wanna sing along
It's about where I belong
Texas

Sometimes far into the night
And until the morning light
I pray with all my might
To be in Texas

It's where I wanna be
It's the only place for me
Where my spirit can be free
Texas

Texans have a reputation for bragging about being the biggest and the best. But that's not the Texas I know. My Texas is a humble place. The city of my birth is a humble village. The people I grew up with are humble souls.

After struggling in Nashville, I returned to Texas in 1970, not as a conquering hero but as just another singer with a band looking to survive. At that point in my life, I was different. I'd given up the clean-cut look and dressed the way I wanted to: jeans and T-shirts. I let my hair grow and quit shaving. I started playing with musicians like Leon Russell, who was considered a hippie. That suited me just fine. Leon was the best entertainer I'd ever encountered. (Leon, by the way, was an Okie.)

When I settled in Austin in the early seventies, I was accepted for who I was. It was the biggest turning point in my professional life. Everyone said the two groups who liked my music, hippies and rednecks, would never get along. But when I started my Fourth of July Picnics, they got along just fine.

"Texas" is a song filled with Spanish guitars because that's the music I grew up with. I grew up with Mexican and Black and Czech people. I grew up in an environment of tolerance.

I'm not saying Texas didn't and doesn't have problems. Bigotry persists. Manipulative politicians trade on racial prejudice. But the Texas I love best is the Texas that respects differences, the Texas where openhearted human beings accept one another and embrace a code of behavior that says live and let live.

July 4, 1973, the first official Dripping Springs Willie Nelson Picnic.

BLUE STAR

You know I'll follow you to the end
Whenever that is, we both will know
How I will follow you again
Anywhere that love can go

If I beat you to the end
I've had a big head start, it's true
And we're just riding on the wind
Still the same old me and you

And when you reach the heavens bright
I'll be the blue star on your right

I knew the first time that I saw you
That an angel had found its way to me
We'll be back together out there drifting
Everywhere as far as we can see

When I was a young man, I loved to listen to old men tell stories. Later, as an old man myself, I turned some of those stories into songs.

The Hill County Courthouse is situated in Hillsboro, Texas, just nine miles north of my hometown of Abbott. It's a magnificent structure from 1890 built of limestone and topped off by a seven-story clock tower.

As a kid I'd sit in Courthouse Square and listen to the old-timers tell stories. One elderly gentleman had memories of the Civil War. But it wasn't the battles he liked to talk about. It was his woman.

He met a gal from Alabama and moved her to Wichita Falls, where he worked at the Zales jewelry store. He set diamonds in rings, bracelets, and pendants. One day when a shipment came in from New York, he spotted a rare blue-colored diamond. He asked his boss, Mr. Zale, if he could use the stone to make a ring for his wife. The jewel was expensive, but Mr. Zale let him pay it out over ten years.

The day he made his final payment, his wife died of a stroke. A few days after her funeral, he sat in his backyard and wept. Wiping away his tears, he looked up at the heavens. He noticed a brilliant blue star. Thinking he might be dreaming, he asked his neighbor to confirm his sighting. "Yes," said the neighbor, "the star is blue."

That same evening, he opened the drawer where his wife kept her jewelry. The ring was there, but the blue-colored diamond wasn't.

"She turned into a star," said the old man, "and it won't be long when I'll be shining up there with her."

Cracking up with my friend, legendary Texas Longhorns coach Darrell Royal.

I'VE GOT A LOT OF TRAVELING TO DO

I've got a lot of traveling to do
Still got a whole lot of traveling left to do
Talk about a mover who has way too much
  to lose
It's time I put back on my rambling shoes
I've got a lot of traveling to do

I've got a lot of traveling to do
A whole lot of traveling left to do
The road is getting crowded and they're
  shortening my fuse
Ain't nothing here I really care to lose
And I got a lot of traveling to do

I've got a lot of traveling to do
And I can't forget the shit you put me
  through
Of course I can forgive you 'cause that's
  just what I do
But I've got some traveling to do

Got a lot of traveling to do
A whole lot of traveling to do
Gonna fire it up and smoke it down
Hello goodbye to you
Light one more and write a song or two

Got a lot of traveling to do

May 28, 1963

My Dearest Children,

Well here I am again. Your great big, fat, ugly daddy missing you very much. It seems that everytime I turn around and every where I look, I see some little boy playing with his ball or little girls dressed up so pretty walking down the street and I think of you.

As you grow older, you will come to realize that things do not always work out exactly as you want them to. There will be many things that you will want more than anything

in the world but for some reason you wont be able to have them, then you may feel badly and think that life has played a dirty trick on you and you will not be able to understand why. But always know and remember what daddy told you, happiness does not come from having everything you want, but in understanding and accepting all, and in prayer and the belief that every thing always happens for the best always.

Write me soon. I am always looking for your letters.

All the Love in the world

Daddy

The road might be an addiction or even affliction, but I don't see it that way. Sure, it gets habitual; and sure, it can be an escape from problems you don't want to face. And sure, the inability to settle down might seem unsettling. But to those of us who've chosen to lead life on the road, we wouldn't have it any other way.

Traveling tries your patience. Traveling tests your stamina. Traveling runs the risk of rotting your brain. But traveling also presents the potential of expanding your brain. Meeting exciting new people in exciting new places can keep you from turning cynical.

Traveling is also an ideal place for putting pen to paper. Traveling songs have the built-in rhythm of the road. When I'm sitting on the bus, watching the country whiz by, I get the itch to stitch together a few lines. I think of guys I've traveled with who, for whatever reasons, have lost their cool and gone off the deep end. I remember other guys who spend all their time complaining about their women back home. Then there are those who get so homesick they go cuddle up in the fetal position and sleep for endless hours.

All these guys, whether forgiving souls, lonely hearts, or spiteful assholes, deserve a song of their own. They're road dogs who howl and bark and whine their way up and down the interstates of life. They're trapped or freed by a lifestyle that, unlike any other, is conducive to creative thinking.

I like the hum of the engine, the sound of the rolling tires, the perpetual motion that makes me think that, just as I'll never run out of new places to see, I'll never run out of new songs to write.

Life on the road can take you away from your family, so I'd write letters to my kids from their "great big, fat, ugly daddy" who missed them very much.

SLOW DOWN OLD WORLD

Slow down, slow down old world
There's no hurry
'Cause my life ain't mine anymore
I lived too fast, now it's too late to worry
And I'm too blue to cry anymore

I once was a fool for the women
Now I'm just a fool, nothing more
So slow down, slow down old world
There's no hurry

'Cause my life ain't mine anymore
I once had a way with the women
Till one got away with my heart
So slow down, slow down old world
There's no hurry
'Cause my life ain't mine anymore

I was always taken with the expression that says, "I'll be with you in a New York minute." It's that hurry-up-no-time-to-waste feeling you get when you're smack in the middle of the city that never sleeps.

During that same period that I was working out stories for *Shotgun Willie*, I was looking out the window of my high-rise hotel. The taxis were honking, the buses belching, the cars weaving in and out of traffic, the pedestrians huffing and puffing like they were late for their own funerals. The tempo was furious, thrilling, and crazy at the same time.

Sometimes I write about what I see right in front of me. Other times I write about what I'd rather see.

I wanted to see the "still" in the city, not everything moving so frantically. I wanted to write about someone who had been caught up in speed, finally realizing that the frantic pace had done him dirty.

For most of my adult life, I was a runner. I did so to keep in shape but also for the pure beauty of the act itself. It feels good to jog through a lush green countryside by day or a deserted metropolis by night. Feels good to get your adrenaline going. But that's exercise. You can't be running all the time.

Modifying your speed and finding life's right rhythm is an art form. I'm not sure I've mastered it. I do know, though, that if I've made a mistake, it's usually those times when, like a cab driver roaring down Broadway, I've tried going too far too quickly.

COME ON TIME

Time is my friend, my friend
And the more I reject it
The more it kicks in
Just enough to keep me on my toes

I say, come on time I've beat you before
Come on time what have you got for me this
   time
I'll take your words of wisdom
And I'll try to make them rhyme

Hey, it's just me and you again
Come on time

Time, you're not fooling me
You're something I can't kill
You're flying like a mighty wind
You're never standing still

Time, as you've passed me by
Why did you leave these lines on my face
You sure have put me in my place
Come on time, come on time
It looks like you're winning the race

Benjamin Franklin said, "Time is money." Ol' Ben was a motivated man who, in his spare time, harnessed electricity while helping write the Constitution and win the Revolutionary War. He used time well.

The majority of us mortals, fixated on making money in a hot hurry, struggle with time. We fear it. We try to outsmart it or outrun it and, of course, we wind up losing the race.

"Come On Time" is another song written in my eighties when I've finally found the sense to surrender. My battle with time is over. My delusions are dead. Even though I'm singing and playing at a fast tempo, the message belies the rhythm. The harder I try to conquer time, the quicker time conquers me.

But at the other end of this dilemma, I find comfort. I find myself believing that, despite the eternal tenacity of time, we really do have all the time in the world. That's because time isn't finite. It goes on forever. Humans have chopped up time in units like seconds and centuries. Those units are arbitrary. The bigger view is that, like the cosmos, time is unimaginably vast. Like the ocean, we can swim in it. Like the sky, we can fly through it. Like love, it has no beginning or ending. It just is.

From the top, Paul, me, Jimmy Day, and David Zettner.

KNEEL AT THE FEET OF JESUS

I guess I been hanging around too long
It's just about time I was moving along
But, I'm gonna kneel at the feet of Jesus in the
  morning
And don't you worry and don't you moan
It's just about time I was moving along

I'm gonna kneel at the feet of Jesus in the
  morning
I'm gonna leave this sinful world before the
  dawning

Just one thing before you carry me away
Don't you bury me deep 'cause I ain't gonna
  stay
I'm gonna kneel at the feet of Jesus in the
  morning
A little bit of dirt and a little bit of gravel
Don't you weigh me down 'cause you know I
  gotta travel

And I'm gonna kneel at the feet of Jesus in the
  morning
I'm gonna leave this sinful world before the
  dawning

Before we move on from "Still Is Still Moving," I want to add this song about two things that don't seem to go together: kneeling and moving on.

"Kneel at the Feet of Jesus" was recorded in 1971 on the first album that carried the name *Willie Nelson & Family.* My first family ties are the deepest, the ones that connect me to my sister and Mama and Daddy Nelson. Those ties are forever connected to the spirit born of music. This song hearkens back to the spirit that washed over the Abbott United Methodist Church where I was raised. (By the way, in 2006 when Bobbie and I heard our childhood church was being torn down, we bought it. It still stands today.)

Kneeling is a humbling process. Puts my ego in check. Acknowledges my acceptance of the Creator. Creativity flows from a higher source filled with love. Conversely, if I'm believing I'm the Be-All-and-End-All of everything, I cut off that flow.

Once I kneel, I don't have to stay down. I get up and move into whatever adventure awaits me on either side of the grave. I'm moving on with joy, I'm moving on with gratitude. Grateful for all I'm leaving behind, grateful for all that lies ahead.

PHASES AND STAGES

In 1974, when Atlantic Records was still underwriting my musical instincts, I put out my second concept album with a simple format: On the first side, a woman tells her story; and on the second, a man takes over. Both sides are about sadness, both about a relationship in ruins.

I'm not writing about myself or any relationship of my own. I take on the perspective of a woman I know only in my imagination and the voice of a man who's the composite of a million men I've met.

Some warned me against the project because *Yesterday's Wine,* my previous concept album, didn't make money. Producer Jerry Wexler pushed me in the opposite direction. "Follow your heart," he said. "The concept is strong."

Jerry put me together with, among others, the Muscle Shoals Rhythm Section—famous for backing Aretha Franklin—and then left me to my own devices.

It remains a musical phase of my life when I was digging deep into the emotional well while working at the Muscle Shoals Sound Studio in Sheffield, Alabama, where I felt perfectly at ease. Muscle Shoals didn't feel that far from my hometown of Abbott. It was kicked-back and country cool.

I'll always remember what Jerry said when his colleagues told him that I should be recording in Nashville, not Muscle Shoals. "Muscle Shoals," they said, "is too R&B for Willie."

"Willie," Wexler shot back, "is too R&B for Nashville."

PHASES AND STAGES (THEME) / WASHING THE DISHES

Phases and stages
Circles and cycles
Seems like we've all seen before
Let me tell you some more

Washing the dishes
Scrubbing the floors
Caring for someone
Who don't care anymore

Learning to hate all the things
That she once loved to do
Like washing his shirts
And never complaining

Except of red stains on the collars
Ironing and crying, crying and ironing
Caring for someone who don't
    care anymore
Someday she'll just walk away

To keep going, we do what we gotta do.

But daily tasks can be deadly. The repetition can drive us nuts. But we get it done because we're committed. Until very recent times, women were forced to deal with the dullest tasks. Their inferior status is a prejudice built deep into human history. Like racism, sexism brings out the worst in all of us. Without realizing it, the perpetrator does as much harm to himself as he does to his victim.

For centuries, couples have been swimming in ignorance.

When the bloom of romance comes off the rose, the flower starts to stink.

It isn't a pretty picture.

But it's real.

As kids, we read fairy tales where everyone lives happily ever after.

In life, we learn pain can be more prevalent than pleasure.

What happens when the pain is too much to bear?

What happens when she no longer wants to wash away the red lipstick stains?

How much more can she take?

I've been lucky enough to work with some great people in the studio, like producer Arif Mardin, musician Doug Sahm, and producer Jerry Wexler.

PHASES AND STAGES (THEME) / WALKIN'

Phases and stages
Circles and cycles
Scenes like we've all seen before
Let me tell you some more

After carefully considering the whole situation
And I stand with my back to the wall
Walking is better than running away
And crawling ain't no good at all

And if guilty is the question, truth is the answer
I've been lying to me all along
There ain't nothing worth saving except one another
And before you'll wake up I'll be gone

My mom had a complicated love life, with lots of ups and downs, but I always felt that, no matter what, she maintained her dignity. Same was true for my sister Bobbie. Strong women inspire me.

When I imagine a woman who has been betrayed, it's easy to envision her going off. It's easy to see her taking those dishes that she just washed and smashing them against the wall.

Yet she keeps her cool. She stops and thinks it through. Unlike so many men, she doesn't act on impulse. She doesn't blow her top. She reflects. Her reflection allows her to realize that, though her man is guilty, and though he's been lying, she's also been lying to herself. She's known about his deceptions for longer than she cares to admit.

Her denial is deep, but her dignity is deeper. Part of her is afraid to leave, but a bigger part of her is determined to stand tall. She won't run and she won't crawl.

She'll pack up and, while he sleeps and dreams of someone else, she sees herself walking out the door.

A new world awaits. She'll try not to look back. She'll try not to think about him. But that won't be easy. There's more on her mind . . .

With Mama Nelson.

PRETEND I NEVER HAPPENED

Pretend I never happened
Erase me from your mind
You will not want to remember
Any love as cold as mine

I'll be leaving in the morning
For a place that I hope I find
All the places must be better
Than the ones I leave behind

But I don't suppose you'll be unhappy
You'll find ways to spend your time
And if you ever think about me
And if I ever cross your mind

Just pretend I never happened
Erase me from your mind
You will not want to remember
Any love as cold as mine

Have you talked to a person who isn't there?

It's a one-sided conversation, but sometimes it's a conversation you can't avoid.

You want to tell your lover—who's fast asleep and can't hear a word you're saying—what to do when he wakes and finds you gone.

You've got a lot to say, but you're not about to get him up and say it to his face. You're too smart to trigger a violent confrontation. Instead, you're going to speak to his unconscious mind.

You want to hurt him, just as he's hurt you. You want to let him know that your love has turned cold. Your love for him is gone, just like you're gone.

Let him suffer. Let him deal with your disappearance.

Don't bother to write out a long explanation. He doesn't deserve it.

In time, he'll find other women. Men always do. But if, by chance, he does think of you, there's only one way to forget you: Imagine you never existed.

Meanwhile, you'll do the same: Imagine he never happened.

But can you actually do that?

Can you erase him from your mind?

You aren't sure. All you know for sure is one thing:

You gotta get out while the getting's good.

SISTER'S COMING HOME / DOWN AT THE CORNER BEER JOINT

Sister's coming home
Mama's gonna let her sleep
The whole day long
Well, the whole day long

Sister's coming home
Mama don't like the man
That done her wrong
Well, that's done her wrong

Sister's coming home
Mama's gonna let her sleep
The whole day long
The mirror's gonna tell her
Just how long she's been gone

Down at the corner beer joint
Dancing to the rock 'n' roll
Sister likes to do it
Lord, sister likes to move her soul

Down at the corner beer joint
Dancing on a hardwood floor
Her jeans fit a little bit tighter
Than they did before

It's never easy walking away, but having somewhere to go—somewhere safe—makes all the difference in the world. In my life, I've been blessed to witness the beautiful mother-daughter bond. Sister Bobbie had such a bond with both our mother and our grandmother.

Mama does more than offer you unconditional love; she also backs your decision to walk away from a dire situation. Her support helps settle your restless mind.

Having been up all night, wrestling with your thoughts, pacing the floor, mulling over your past, present, and future, you're a wreck. You gotta sleep.

Sleep comes quickly. Sleeping in your childhood bed brings you just the comfort your exhausted soul needs. The sleep is peaceful. No scary thoughts, no nightmares.

You wake refreshed. You don't want to think of him. You don't want to think at all. You want music. Music lightens your burdens and makes you want to move. Makes you want to dance. You want to dance the way you danced before he ever came along.

If your jeans don't fit the way they used to, who cares?

The barroom is bustling. People are partying. People are welcoming you. You're dancing like you don't have a care in the world.

You're finally feeling free.

In my life, I've been blessed to witness the beautiful mother-daughter bond.

(HOW WILL I KNOW) I'M FALLING IN LOVE

I'm falling in love again
I never thought I would again
I never thought I would

And I may be making mistakes again
But if I lose or win
How will I know?

I'm falling in love again
I never thought I would again
I never thought I would

And I may be making mistakes again
But if I lose or win
How will I know?

The rebound. The bounce back. The recovery.

How long does it take to get your senses back? How long does it take to start thinking straight again?

You're cautious. You meet him at the café for coffee. He doesn't ply you with questions. At the same time, he doesn't need to talk about himself. His voice is soothing. His eyes are soft. No signs of arrogance. Only signs of tenderness. You want to say that his heart is good.

But who are you to say?

You don't like being alone. You like being with him. He's not making a move, and neither are you. He's patient.

Have another cup of coffee. Share a piece of apple pie. Look outside. The sun's starting to set, the blue sky fading to pink.

You've been blue too long. You've missed the way it feels to fall in love.

This is how it feels. He's as sweet as the apple pie. He's someone you can love.

But so was the one you walked away from. You thought you loved him. You thought that love was real.

Is this a new or old reality?

Are you about to lose or win?

Can you afford to gamble?

Can you afford not to?

You've missed the way it feels to fall in love.

BLOODY MARY MORNING

Well, it's a bloody Mary morning
Baby left me without warning
Sometime in the night
So I'm flying down to Houston
Forgetting her the nature of my flight

As we taxi toward the runway
With the smog and haze
Reminding me of how I feel
Just a country boy who's learning
That the pitfalls of the city are extremely real

All the nightlife and the parties
And temptation and deceit
The order of the day
Well, it's a bloody Mary morning
'Cause I'm leaving baby somewhere in LA

Our golden jet is airborne
And flight fifty cuts a path across the
    morning sky
And a voice comes through the speaker
Reassuring us flight fifty is the way to fly

And a hostess takes our order
Coffee, tea or something stronger to start the
    day
Well, it's a bloody Mary morning
'Cause I'm leaving baby somewhere in LA

Whiling away the time on the bus. At least this one isn't broken down.

Now the man reacts the way men often do.

Fright leads to flight.

Don't linger and try to understand what happened. Just get your ass up and out. Book the first thing smoking. Get the hell out of Dodge. LA's deadlier than Dodge. Leaving LA is something you should have done long ago.

Feels good to get on the plane. Feels even better as it lifts off, leaving all that mess behind.

You don't want to remember. You want to forget. Forget the crazy nights and the crazy moves that felt right but turned out wrong. Forget how happy turned sad. How the double life and the double mind doubled your trouble until you found yourself living a lie that you worked overtime to conceal.

Well, that's all good and gone. Good to be flying thirty-three thousand feet above the ground. Good to be suspended in air. Suspended in time. Good to feel the effects of spicy tomato juice and hundred-proof Smirnoff.

"Would you like another?" she asks.

You can't say "yes" quick enough.

NO LOVE AROUND

Phases and stages
Circles and cycles
Scenes like we've all seen before
Let me tell you some more

I come home last Saturday morning
I come home and found you gone
There was a note tacked on my door
Said, "Your baby don't love you anymore"

Well, I got dressed up and I went downtown
I got dressed up and I went downtown
I walked up and I walked down
There weren't no love, there weren't no love around

Well, I come home and I lay down
I felt my head spinning round and round
Lord, I poured my dreams and I drank 'em down
'Cause there weren't no love, there weren't no love around

Variations on the same story.

It's a Friday night. All week you've worked like a dog. The paycheck isn't what you expected. Deductions you don't even understand. But what can you do? You pocket it and cash it and come to a fork in the road.

One direction is well-known. Home. Home makes sense.

The other direction is unknown. Unknown makes for excitement.

You head for unknown excitement. The bar is busting at the seams. The band is blasting. Ladies dancing without partners. One lady looks your way. Her eyes are smiling. Her lips are beckoning. A warning voice inside you says, "No." But after two beers the first voice is silenced by second voice that says, "Yes."

She's a stranger who says, "I feel like I've known you all my life."

You say, "Well, maybe you have."

You're both lying, but lying lets you slip the predictable to a place of unpredictability.

The new life is short-lived. At break of dawn, you leave the motel room. Your head is throbbing with a hangover that has you forgetting what, only hours earlier, seemed like unforgettable pleasure.

Back home, you stumble inside and find the note.

You shower, you change, you go back out, you go back home, you crash on the couch, you look for the love that you chased away, the same love you'll be chasing for days, for months, for years. Maybe forever.

You're both lying, but lying lets you slip the predictable to a place of unpredictability.

I STILL CAN'T BELIEVE YOU'RE GONE

It's the very first day since you left me
But I tried to put my thoughts in a song
And all I can hear myself singing is
I still can't believe you're gone

I still can't believe that you'd leave me
What did I do that was so wrong
There's just too many unanswered questions
And I still can't believe you're gone

But you're gone and I'm alone
And I'm still living
I don't like it but I'll take it
Till I'm strong

And all I can hear myself singing is
I still can't believe you're gone

this is the very first day since you left me
that I've tried to put my thoughts in a song
and all I can hear myself singing
is I still can't believe your gone.
I still can't believe you'd leave me
What did I do that was so wrong
there are too many questions unanswered -
and I still can't believe your gone -
But you gone and I'm still here so I'll keep
living -
I don't like it but I'll take it till I'm strong
But oh it's been so long now darling -
and I still can't believe your gone.

Phases and Stages **is about a fictitious couple.** At the same time as I was writing these songs, though, something happened in real life—an unforeseen tragedy—that shook the Family band. By coincidence, the tragic circumstances fit into the make-believe storyline I was in the process of putting together.

The real-life story is that Carlene, the wife of my best friend Paul English, took her own life. There were no signs or warnings. Those of us close to Carlene loved her dearly. We were devastated. Paul was nearly destroyed. I worried whether he would ever recover. When someone is dealing with that kind of unspeakable pain, you want to do something, anything, to help. You sit by their side. You hug them if they want to be hugged. But mainly you stay silent because you know words don't matter.

In my case, the best thing I could do was write a song. I'd written songs about my buddy before—"Me and Paul" and "Devil in a Sleeping Bag"—but they were fun-loving. This one had to be the saddest song I'd ever written.

Before I recorded it, I felt like I needed Paul's okay. The last thing I wanted to do was invade his privacy. It wasn't easy singing it to him, but I made it through. His eyes were wet with tears. Mine as well. There was a long silence before Paul could speak. When he did, he said only two words:

"Thank you."

IT'S NOT SUPPOSED TO BE THAT WAY

It's not supposed to be that way
You're supposed to know that I love you
But it don't matter anyway
If I can't be there to control you

Like the other little children
You're gonna dream a dream or two
But be careful what you're dreaming
Or soon your dreams will be dreaming you

It's not supposed to be that way
You're supposed to know that I love you
But it don't matter anyway
If I can't be there to console you

When you go out to play this evening
Play with fireflies till they're gone
Then rush to meet your lover
And play with real fire till the dawn

But it's not supposed to be that way
You're supposed to know that I love you
But it don't matter anyway
If I can't be there to console you

Big difference between controlling and consoling.

The man who is left alone finds himself unable to forget. Even though he's not given to reflection, he can't help himself. He can't get her off his mind.

He thinks about controlling her. Controlling the pain that he caused. Controlling her anger. Controlling her decision. Controlling her very soul.

But she's out of his control. Out of his life. And even if she were there, controlling wouldn't work. Controlling never does.

But at least he could console. He could say he's sorry. Express remorse. Offer comfort. But, like controlling, consoling isn't possible when she's long gone and isn't looking back.

There's so much he wants her to know: that he still loves her and cares; that he's learned from the past and is ready to let go, give up control, allow her the freedom to be who she wants to be.

But whoever she is, she's no longer his. It's hard not to fantasize about her and another man. Such fantasies burn through his brain.

It no longer matters. It can't be fixed. It's not supposed to be that way, but it is.

Lana tending
to my hair
while I'm on
the phone.

HEAVEN AND HELL

Sometimes it's heaven and sometimes it's hell
Sometimes I don't even know
Sometimes I take it as far as I can
And sometimes I don't even go

My front tracks are bound for a cold water well
And my back tracks are covered with snow
Sometimes it's heaven and sometimes it's hell
And sometimes I don't even know

In heaven I ain't walking on a street paved
  with gold
And hell ain't no mountain of fire
Heaven is laying in my sweet baby's arms
And hell is when my baby is not there

My front tracks are bound for a cold water well
My back tracks are covered with snow
Sometimes it's heaven and sometimes it's hell
And sometimes I don't even know

Heaven is the past. Hell is the present. The future is a clash between the two. The clash gives no indication of ending anytime soon. It lasts as long as a song. And though a song may be short, the memory can last a lifetime.

My man is stewing in his own juices. He's not thinking of a heaven with angels singing or a hell with fires burning. He's caught between cold and heat, the cold of missing her warm body and the hot memory of the touch of her skin.

Pulled apart. Split in two. Cut in half.

He wants to be whole, but it ain't happening. At the same time, he's moving forward and backward. His head is howling; his heart is hungering.

He says he doesn't know, but he does.

It's her.

He can try to rationalize and reason, try to finagle and forget, but the pain only worsens.

It's her.

It's always her.

The cold of
missing her
warm body
and the hot
memory of
the touch
of her skin.

PICK UP THE TEMPO

People are saying that time will take
    care of people like me
That I'm living too fast and they say I
    can't last for much longer
But little they see that their thoughts
    of me is my savior
And little they know that the beat
    oughta go just a little faster

Pick up the tempo just a little and take
    it on home
The singer ain't singing and the
    drummer's been dragging too long
Time will take care of itself so just
    leave time alone
And pick up the tempo just a little and
    take it on home

I'm wild and I'm mean I'm creating a
    scene I'm going crazy
I'm good and I'm bad and I'm happy
    and I'm sad and I'm lazy
I'm quiet and I'm loud and I'm
    gathering a crowd and I like gravy
About half off the wall but I learned it
    all in the Navy

So pick up the tempo just a little and
    take it on home
The singer ain't singing and the
    drummer's been dragging too long
Time will take care of itself so just
    leave time alone
And pick up the tempo just a little and
    take it on home

Can this story have a happy ending?

Will the couple be reunited and finally find a way forward?

The man would like to think so but knows better. Too much damage has been done.

So what can he do to keep from drowning in his own tears?

Find another rhythm to set him right. Sing another song that doesn't have to make sense. A nonsense song. A song that says he's been saved by thoughts of people who don't think he's gonna last much longer.

That's okay. Let them think whatever they wanna. He'll be whoever he is. He'll stop trying to put together the pieces. There's no reconciling the differences. Like bumper cars at the Texas State Fair, let the contradictions crash head-on. Let the inconsistencies grow more inconsistent.

What matters is movement. Tell the band to get busy. Wake up the drummer. The beat needs a boost. Go on and kick the singer's ass.

Kick him from one phase to another. From one stage to the next.

Phases and Stages is over, except it's not. It's just the snippet of a story. The big story never stops.

WHERE *do you* STAND?

Mama Nelson taught me to avoid antagonizing people. She taught me to consider other folks' points of view. I've tried adopting that attitude, but I also believe in speaking my mind. When I believe in something strongly, I also believe in putting it into song. Some say keep politics out of music. That's like saying keep politics out of life. Politics affects everyone. So does music. That's why we need songs that remind us that burying our heads in the ground like ostriches won't solve a thing.

If I write one song that consoles, I better write another that challenges. I don't want to get complacent. And I sure don't want to get jaded. I want to give you my point of view. I'm not claiming to be an expert or sage. But I am someone who does his fair share of thinking. And because I've always had a platform—whether singing to forty folks or forty thousand—I feel compelled to use that platform responsibly.

If you don't agree with me, fine. And if my political positions get you so angry you won't buy my records or come to my shows, no worries. No one can please everyone all the time. All we can do is say and sing what matters to us and let the chips fall where they may.

WHERE DO YOU STAND?

I'm somewhere behind you
You've come with your suitcase in hand
Hey, what's your plan, where do you stand?

The world's still divided
And you're still undecided, decide if you can
Hey, what's your plan, where do you stand?

It's time for commitments
It's time for a showing of hands
Hey, what's your plan, where do you stand?

Surely there's someone with courage
To say where he stands
Hey, what's your plan, where do you stand?

You probably haven't heard of Gatewood Galbraith. He was a smart, big-hearted attorney from Lexington, Kentucky, with a thriving practice in criminal and personal injury law. I got to know him in the nineties when he threw his hat in the gubernatorial race. A key part of his platform was the legalization of pot. When he called to ask whether I'd campaign for him, I was quick to say, "Hell, yes."

Gatewood was a stalwart. Like me, he believed in the power of hemp. In fact, when we crisscrossed the state—him making speeches, me singing songs—his Cadillac was fueled by hemp oil.

As a witness to the positive attributes of marijuana, I was happy to jump on the bandwagon. It was an opportunity to educate the public. I was with him the two times he entered the Democratic primary. Unfortunately, he lost both races. An indefatigable soul, he switched to the Reform Party and ran again.

"Willie," he said, "this third run will be another losing proposition. I know you may be losing fans. I'll understand if you'd rather sit it out."

"I'd rather bring it on," I said. "Let's roll."

As a third-party candidate, the good counselor did do a bit better. He got fifteen percent of the vote.

At the end of the day, though, he knew what I knew: The legalization of marijuana was coming. It was only a matter of time.

If you don't agree with me, fine.

VOTE 'EM OUT

If you don't like who's in there, vote 'em out
That's what election day is all about
The biggest gun we've got
Is called the ballot box

So if you don't like who's in there
Vote 'em out, vote 'em out
And when they're gone we'll sing and dance
   and shout

Bring some new ones in
And we'll start that show again
And if you don't like who's in there, vote 'em
   out

If it's a bunch of clowns you voted in
Election day is coming round again
If you don't like it now
If it's more than you'll allow

If you don't like who's in there
Vote 'em out, vote 'em out
And when they're gone we'll sing and dance
   and shout

Bring some new ones in
And we'll start the show again
And if you don't like who's in there,
   vote 'em out

I call it anger therapy. I get pissed off and write my anger out in a song.

One thing that pisses me off royally is hearing people bitch and moan about the politicians—and then not bother to vote. Voting is a sacred privilege. Not voting is a sacrilege.

I wrote this song on a balmy night in Maui and wasn't sure when I'd get to sing it. The opportunity popped up in a hurry. Beto O'Rourke was running for senator in 2018. He'd won the Democratic primary by a big margin and was facing the Republican. I saw Beto as a young populist with strong progressive views. So when he asked me to come to his rally in Austin, I said sure.

Sixty thousand souls showed up at Austin's Auditorium Shores, hard by the Colorado River. I turned up in a Beto baseball cap and Beto T-shirt. I was all in. Beto urged me to do a whole set. I kept it short. We did "Whiskey River," "Mamas Don't Let Your Babies Grow Up to Be Cowboys," and a couple of others. But the song that got 'em going, the one they seemed to be waiting for, was the one no one had ever heard before.

Yet by the time I hit the second chorus of "Vote 'Em Out," they were singing along like they knew the song better than me.

I think I'd vote for a Waylon and Johnny ticket.

JIMMY'S ROAD

This is Jimmy's road where Jimmy liked to play
This is Jimmy's grass where Jimmy liked to lay around

This is Jimmy's tree where Jimmy liked to climb
But Jimmy went to war and something changed his mind around

This is the battleground where Jimmy learned to kill
Now Jimmy has a trade and Jimmy knows it well too well

This is Jimmy's grave where Jimmy's body lies
And when a soldier falls Jimmy's body dies and dies

But this is Jimmy's road where Jimmy likes to play
This is Jimmy's grass where Jimmy likes to lay around

The sixties was a decade like no other. I loved the peace movement. I loved the boldly creative music emerging from every genre, from country to rock to soul to blues. I loved the psychedelic flavor in the air. There was a sense that the world might really be reborn for the better. But then there was the brutality of Vietnam.

In the midst of what looked like a renewal of the human spirit, America found itself bogged down in an unwinnable war. It was a futile cause where millions of soldiers and civilians alike lost their lives. War is always tragic, even those with a supposedly noble purpose. But when you're fighting for reasons that no one, especially those doing the fighting, understands, you can't help but despair.

I wrote "Jimmy's Road" when the war was still raging. My friend and bandmate David Zettner served in Vietnam and came home with horror stories. Listening to David inspired this story. While I did have Vietnam in mind, Jimmy could have been killed in any war in any country in any time in history.

Human beings are capable of great acts of kindness. At the same time, we turn on each other with murderous intent. We become barbarians. We slaughter and maim. We vilify our enemies and, under the guise of self-protection, we inflict horrific damage.

I pray that the spirit of the sixties that said "make love not war" will prevail again—and there comes a day when no one has to travel down Jimmy's Road.

BAND OF BROTHERS

We're a band of brothers and sisters and
    whatever
On a mission to break all the rules
And I know you love me 'cause I love you too
But you can't tell me what to do

And I sure don't know where we're going
I'm really not sure where we've been
But if I can take you all with me
I'd sure like to go there again

'Cause we're a band of brothers and sisters and
    whatever
On a mission to break all the rules
And I know you love me 'cause I love you too
But you can't tell me what to do

When all of the songs have been written
And when all of the music is played
When the curtain comes down
We'll still be around to make sure the
    musicians are paid

Can't explain why, but I was born a rebel. I've remained a rebel and I'm guessing I'll be reincarnated a rebel as well.

Been ten years or so since I wrote this song. I was charging headfirst into my eighties. Figured it was time to restate my feeling about my brothers, my sisters, and, to use my favorite word in the song, my "whatever" friends.

I like living in a world where the old categories are not only being challenged but being busted wide open. The old rules that kept folks in little boxes were cruel rules. People suffered because society condemned differences. Society is afraid of differences. Society sucks—at least the society that perpetuates conformity.

I grew up in the forties and fifties. I suffered, often silently, through an era where the mantra was go-along-to-get-along. I tried to fit in. My attempts were futile. I couldn't be someone I wasn't. There's only one me, just like there's only one you. Like the song says, I may not know where I've been or where I'm going, but I do know I want to get back to the essence of my mixed-up nature.

Being mixed up, embracing the wild blend of elements that constitute who we are, can be a good thing. If more of us copped to uncertainty, we wouldn't have to stake out these obstinate do-or-die positions. We could be more flexible, more willing to listen to others. We'd have a better chance of being a band of brothers and sisters and whatever.

"Whatever" is whatever you want it to be.

Neil Young and John Mellencamp have never been shy about their political views.

BRING IT ON

They say there is no gain without pain
Well, I must be gaining a lot
And I'll give it all that I got to bring it on

It seems that I've been here before
So if this means that there is more
Bring it on

It's written in the Good Book
That we'll never be asked
To take any more than we can
Sounds like a good plan
So bring it on

"If I can't see it or feel it
I don't worry," said someone
And I'll have to say I agree
Bring it on

Well, I know you're out there
'Cause I hear you breathing
But it still don't mean nothing to me
So bring it on

Bring it on, bring it on
It's just one more storm in the sea
Bring it on

Another song that came to mind as I entered my eighties,

"Bring It On" surprised me with its defiant tone. Wasn't anything I planned. It just came out that way.

Sometimes I sound braver in my songs than I feel in real life. This might be an instance where I wrote a song to shore up my bravery. The spirit of music is the source of my courage. As long as I'm able, I'll never stop making music, because I'll never stop needing courage.

Going through this life without losing your mind is no easy trick. Fighting off negative thoughts can be a full-time job. To wage that battle, I need to utilize my full arsenal.

Rather than shrink from the forces conspiring to freak you out, it might not be a bad idea to call them out. They tend to lurk in the dark corners of your mind. But if you coax them out so you can look at them in the light of day, they're not so scary.

Bring on the monsters. Bring on the bad guys. Bring on the boogie man. Bring on the voices inside your head that say there's nothing but nightmares ahead.

Bring on everything you fear. Line up the fears. Face the fears and then laugh. Then smile. Then realize that the fears are figments of your imagination.

Bring 'em on and watch 'em fade away.

Bob Dylan was kind enough to stop by my 60th birthday party, "The Big Six-O."

HEARTLAND

There's a home place under fire tonight in
the heartland
And the bankers are taking my home and
my land from me

There's a big gaping hole in my chest now
where my heart was
And a hole in the sky where God used to be

There's a home place under fire tonight in
the heartland
There's a well where the water's so bitter
nobody can drink

Ain't no way to get high and my mouth is so
dry that I can't speak
Don't they know that I'm dying why's
nobody crying for me

My American dream fell apart at the seams
You tell me what it means
You tell me what it means

There's a home place under fire tonight in
the heartland
And bankers are taking the homes and the
land away

There's a young boy closing his eyes tonight
in the heartland
Who will wake up a man with some land
and a loan he can't pay

His American dream fell apart at the seams
You tell me what it means
You tell me what it means

I wrote this song with Bob Dylan in 1990, but its roots go back to 1985 when Bob and I were talking after a Live Aid concert. He mentioned that doing a concert for the small farmers all over America might be a good thing. Then I brought the idea to Illinois governor Jim Thompson, who, within months, made it happen. Neil Young and John Mellencamp became prime movers and suddenly there we all were—me, Bob, Neil, John, Waylon, Merle, Charley Pride, Johnny Cash, Bonnie Raitt, Loretta Lynn, Kris Kristofferson, Billy Joel, B.B. King, and many others—performing in front of eighty thousand fans at Memorial Stadium in Champaign. Thirty-seven years later, the all-day annual event is still going strong.

Bob and I shared the same view—the fact that the small farmer was getting screwed was infuriating. The small farmer was an unsung hero.

I can't remember what lyrics and notes Bob wrote and which were mine. Doesn't matter. We were of one mind. The flow came easy and I'm not sure there was a single edit. When we finally recorded as a duet in 1993, that flow was still there. We sang a story that, although heartbreaking, needed to be told.

To give voice to the voiceless is a priceless privilege that comes with being a writer.

DELETE AND FAST FORWARD

Delete and fast forward, my friend
The wars are all over and nobody wins
But don't worry too much, just drive you crazy
    again
So delete and fast forward, my friend

Delete and fast forward, my son
The elections are over and nobody won
You think it's all ending but it's just setting in
So delete and fast forward, my friend

Delete and fast forward again
It's just one big circle and it's beginning to end
What's next was now and what's now is now
    again
So delete and fast forward again

Delete and fast forward the news
The truth is the truth but believe what you
    choose
When we blow the whole world back to where
    it began
Just delete and fast forward again

Had a chance to be brilliant and we blew it
    again
So delete and fast forward, my friend

One of the many songs I wrote with my good buddy Buddy Cannon in the past decade, "Delete and Fast Forward" triggered all kinds of responses.

"Willie's turned cynical."

"Willie believes the Last Days are approaching."

"Willie's giving up on political change."

"Willie's jaded."

"Willie's buying into fake news."

"Willie's stopped even trying to make his songs make sense."

The last comment is my favorite. The others don't bother me at all. Let people say what they want to say about my songs. Long as they keep listening to them, I'm fine.

The fact is, I do believe that when I delete and fast forward I'm actually getting somewhere. I'm doing away with all negative energy and recharging my batteries. That's a daily necessity.

If I had dwelled on the *could've*s and *should've*s, I would have aggravated myself into an early grave. Regret begets misery. Forgetting ain't a bad thing. Remembering to keep moving is a good thing.

I like hitting that delete key. But I also like hitting those other keys that, before I know it, have turned my nonsense into a new song.

Governor Jim Thompson, the Farm Aid facilitator.

I'LL TRY TO DO BETTER NEXT TIME

I been sitting around counting my blessings
Thinking of friends here and gone
Recalling the smile across somebody's face
Whenever I'd sing her a song

The Good Book says, "Love everybody"
And the Lord knows I really have tried
So I'll throw a kiss to the ones that I have
    missed
And I'll try to do better next time

By next time I might be a preacher
Or an eagle gliding away
I hope that my spirit will make someone happy
When I'm gone to come back again

The Good Book says, "Love everybody"
And the Lord knows I really have tried
So I'll throw a kiss to the ones that I have
    missed
And I'll try to do better next time

I could not have written this song as a young man. It took a long life to get these lines out of me. And if it doesn't exactly express the same attitude of the previous song, "Delete and Fast Forward," that's fine. I got all kinds of attitudes running through my brain.

This attitude says that there are things I could have done that I didn't. Political things. Personal things. Professional things. There are relationships I ruined and tried to repair. Sometimes the repair job worked, sometimes it failed. There are people I could have treated better and situations I wish I had handled differently.

What keeps me from getting depressed is the notion that there will be a next time.

I recently stumbled upon something that Jack London, author of the classic *The Call of the Wild*, wrote: "I did not begin when I was born nor when I was conceived. I have been growing, developing, through incalculable myriads of millenniums. . . . All my previous selves have their voices, echoes, promptings in me. . . . Oh, incalculable times again shall I be born."

I agree with Jack, and the next time I'll try to do better.

Neil Young was instrumental in making Farm Aid happen.

BURNED BRIDGES

It can feel good to feel bad—at least in songs. One of the biggest hits I ever had was "Blue Eyes Crying in the Rain." Fred Rose wrote it. Roy Acuff sang it in 1947, Hank Williams did it in 1951, and I tackled it in 1975. The sadness inherent in that song is timeless. I'd also call the sadness beautiful because it's so sincere.

I heard the Acuff version when I was fourteen, and although my life experience was limited, I got it. I understood the power of telling stories of love gone bad. I also understood that's a story with a thousand and one variations. Folks never tire of stories they recognize as true, stories that reflect what they themselves have gone through.

If you called these story-songs another form of the blues, I wouldn't argue. They're all about revealing wounds and hoping for healing.

Today, a happy man with a happy marriage, I still find myself writing about unhappiness. It isn't anything I do intentionally. It's just a well of feelings that hasn't run dry and, I suspect, never will.

ONE MORE SONG TO WRITE

I got one more song to write
And I've got one more bridge to burn
I've got one more endless night
One more lesson to be learned

One more hill to climb
And it's somewhere in my mind
I'll know it when it's right
I've got one more song to write

I got one more horse to ride
And no more secrets left to hide
No more staring at the sun
Just to watch them ponies run

No more bounty to divide
There ain't no secrets left to hide
My life's an open book
Turn the page and have a look

I got one more song to write
I've got one more bridge to burn
I've got one more endless night
One more lesson to be learned

Case in point:

I wrote "One More Song to Write" only a few years back. When I played it for a lifelong pal, he said, "Willie, you're singing like you've lost your best friend."

"Haven't I always sung that way?"

"When you were younger, you sounded happier."

"Maybe because I didn't know any better."

"So what's got you down these days?"

"Nothing," I said. "Feeling fine. Feeling strong. Feeling like there's a still a future. Another song to sing."

"But this song says you got another bridge to burn. What bridge?"

"Who knows?"

"You should know, Willie, you wrote the damn thing."

"Just 'cause I wrote it doesn't mean I know what it's about."

"That's crazy."

"'Crazy' might have been my biggest seller. When folks ask me to explain it, I say I can't."

"I can."

"Go ahead," I said.

"Willie is a crazy man who can't stop writing sad songs."

"That's as good an explanation as any."

I never could pull off that outfit as well as Charley Pride.

LITTLE THINGS

I hope I won't disturb you with this call
I'm just in town for such a little while
And I thought perhaps you'd like to hear the news

Jeannie's grades were the highest in the school
Billy sure does look a lot like you
I understand your other son does too

And Billy said, "Tell Mom I miss her so"
These were some little things
I thought you'd like to know

Remember Sam and Peg who lived next door
With them it seemed we always laughed so much
Well, Sam and Peg don't live there anymore

I understand they broke up just like us
The house we lived in now has been torn down
Of all the things we owned the last to go

A freeway now runs through that part of town
These were some little things
That I thought you'd like to know

Not all nightmares are about bloody monsters chasing us down dark alleys. Sometimes the quietest nightmare is the most frightening. One nightmare was so silently scary that when I woke up in the morning I was still shaking. To lose the shakes, I had to reshape it into a song.

I meet and marry my childhood sweetheart, our hearts filled with love. I see our little home. The lace curtains covering the windows. The blue and yellow flowers blooming in the front yard. The sounds of singing birds by our bedroom. The little things.

I remember building the deck in our backyard. The barbecues. The kids growing up as we grew apart. That certain faraway look on your face as you sat alone, making a sweater, reading a book, or sweetly staring into space.

The fear I felt in the pit of my stomach. The knowledge that the future was behind us. The certainty that the dream had become a nightmare.

The exact hour on the kitchen clock—11:43 p.m.—when you told me you were no longer mine. The rainstorm that broke on the day we worked out the arrangements in the lawyer's office. The name of the moving truck—Acme Haulers. The sound of the kids crying. The soggy spaghetti dinner I made them that first night you were gone.

I didn't want to tell you about this nightmare. I didn't want to disturb you.

But there are a few things I want you to know. Nothing big. Just little things that linger in my mind. And I can't help but wonder if these little things linger in your mind as well.

Sometimes the quietest nightmare is the most frightening.

ONCE MORE
WITH FEELING

Once more with feeling, once more with feeling
Won't you hold me till the night fades into day
Once more with feeling, once more with feeling
Hold me close don't let this feeling go away

Sometimes myself runs back to you
I just can't tell me what to do
But I remember when all wrapped up tight
Within the shelter of my arms you used to say

Once more with feeling, once more with feeling
Won't you hold me till the night fades into day
Once more with feeling, once more with feeling
Hold me close don't let this feeling go away

I can be anywhere—Abbott, Texas, or Amsterdam, Netherlands. It can be dead-cold winter or scorching-hot summer. I can be feeling great after a delicious meal or dealing with nasty all-night indigestion. I can be on a mellow high or fighting back the blues. My mood doesn't matter. At any time, in any place, no matter my condition, an image will assault me.

I see the face of a woman.

She has no name.

I know her intimately, but I don't know her at all.

She's always been there.

I've tried to forget her. I can't.

There are a million stories attached to her, and yet she exists apart from any story. She just is. We look at each other for a long, long time. We can't avert our eyes. We don't know what to say. We don't even know who we are.

All we know is that something has vanished. Something is gone that can't be retrieved. Something lost forever.

I hear her breathing. I hear my own breath. My breath carries four words that keep repeating like a mantra.

Once more with feeling.

What is the feeling?

Yearning. Deep, deep yearning.

SAD SONGS AND WALTZES

I'm writing a song all about you
A true song as real as my tears
But you've no need to fear it
'Cause no one will hear it
'Cause sad songs and waltzes
Aren't selling this year

I'll tell all about how you cheated
I'd like for the whole world to hear
I'd like to get even with you
'Cause you're leaving
But sad songs and waltzes
Aren't selling this year

It's a good thing that I'm not a star
You don't know how lucky you are
And though my record may say it
No one will play it
'Cause sad songs and waltzes
Aren't selling this year

I was speaking with Arif Mardin, who was producing some of the songs on my *Shotgun Willie* album. It was 1973, and we were in the Atlantic Records studio in New York City. A kind and sophisticated gentleman born in Istanbul, Arif was a great arranger who had worked with everyone from Aretha Franklin to Bette Midler.

When I sang him "Sad Songs and Waltzes," his first response was a broad smile followed by a little laugh.

Since it was a sad song, I wasn't sure why he was laughing.

"I'm laughing in appreciation," said Arif, the ultimate diplomat. "You've written a song that says it will never sell."

"It probably won't," I said.

"You've composed a double-reverse revenge song where you claim that no one—not even the object of your wrath—will ever hear it. At the same, the whole purpose of the song is to broadcast your fury."

"You make it sound complicated, Arif."

"You're complicated, Willie! You write a song that you label unfashionable and unmarketable in the hopes it will be just the opposite. Am I understanding you?"

"As much as anyone can ever understand me."

Producer Arif Mardin, sister Bobbie, and Paul English join me in the studio as we record the album *Shotgun Willie*.

I MADE A MISTAKE

I made a mistake, Lord, I thought I was wronged
I said, "Take it then, and git," she said, "Got it, and gone"
So I'm writing it all down in this stupid ol' song
I made a mistake, Lord, I thought I was wronged

I'm a lot like Ol' Ripley and I'll believe it or not
I told a big lie, Lord, and then I forgot
I thought I was Jesus and believe me, I'm not
I thought I was right and I was wrong by a lot

I feel a little like Elvis when he was alone
I made another mistake, Lord, I thought I was wronged

I made a mistake, Lord, and it's all on me
I wouldn't admit it but it's easy to see
So if anyone's praying, a request I would make
Is to mention my name 'cause I made a mistake

A song that, although written when I was eighty-four, could have been written when I was fourteen.

If I wanted to be fancy, I'd say, "It was a matter of miscommunication." But in truth, I just fucked up.

Not me, mind you, but the poor soul living the story I custom-wrote just for him.

He's one of those fools who act purely on impulse.

Unlike me.

He's a guy who, in dealing with women, constantly loses his cool.

Unlike me.

He's someone who, when it comes to romance, is not above playing two hands at once.

Unlike me.

He's stubborn, willful, and self-centered.

Unlike me.

And unlike me, he's determined to look good even when he does bad.

Looking to cover up a multitude of sins, he'll even write a song to rationalize his misbehavior.

Unlike me.

But in truth, I just fucked up.

GUITAR IN THE CORNER

There's a guitar in the corner
That used to have a song
I would hold it while it played me
And I would sing along

There was a happy song about her
Loving me like I loved her
But the strings no longer ring
And things are not the way they were

Now when I need a song
My mind goes back where I belong
When I'm not there
And the future is not clear
And the past is just a smoke ring in the air

And that guitar in the corner
Just waits there by the wall
Standing guard and thinking
A new song might come to call

And free us from this minor key
That we both been living in
And we'll pick up where we left off
And play some songs again

There's a guitar in the corner
That used to have our songs
I would hold it when I played it
And I would sing along

Anthropomorphism.

There it is. The biggest word I'm going to use in this book. I'm not using it to impress you, but only for me to remember what it means. Someone used it the other day. I liked the way it sounded, looked it up, and saw how it fit this particular song.

Anthropomorphism isn't anything more than putting human traits on nonhuman things. Cartoon characters like Mickey Mouse and Donald Duck are good examples. The best example is Trigger, the guitar in the corner.

Trigger is the most precious nonhuman object I own. Sometimes it feels like Trigger owns me. Sometimes it feels like Trigger *is* me. I've got crevices in my face. So does Trigger. He has too many knicks and cracks to count. Trigger is alive.

In my solitary moments with Trigger, I play songs by my hero, Django Reinhardt, the genius guitarist. I try to play at least one of Django's songs, like "Nuages," in every show. When he was a teenager, Django burned his hand so badly that, for all practical purposes, he basically could play only with two fingers. He did more with those two fingers than anyone in history. A member of Norah Jones's band, the Little Willies, said that I play like Django, only with one finger. Man, that's the nicest compliment I've ever gotten.

Trigger is the most precious nonhuman object I own.

WHERE DREAMS COME TO DIE

This is where dreams come to die
This is where dreams come to die
Then they fly back to heaven
But this is where dreams come to die

They're fun when you dream them
And everyone's laughing at you
And it's fun watching them wonder
When all of the dreams are coming true

This is where dreams come to die
This is where dreams come to die
Then they fly back to heaven
But this is where dreams come to die

This world is just a stopover
On their journey up to the sky
And here's to the trip back to heaven
May they be safe as they fly

This is where dreams come to die
Then they fly back to heaven
But this is where dreams come to die

I have a soft spot in my heart for this dreamy song of mine.

That's because it was among the last things I recorded with Merle Haggard, a man I admired and loved. Brother Merle was one of the greats. We cut an album in 2015 called *Django and Jimmie*, an homage to my guitar hero and to Jimmie Rodgers, who inspired me, Merle, and every country singer who's ever lived.

I want to show off and use that "anthropomorphism" word again. I'm thinking it applies to what Merle and I were singing. I see dreams as characters in a story. They move around like lost souls. They have minds of their own. Sometimes I feel like I can touch my dreams. Sometimes they escape me. Some dreams I've dreamed for decades. Others are as fresh as this morning's hot coffee.

When we got through singing the song, Merle was moved.

"Willie," he said, "I love what you wrote about dreams, but I don't believe they ever do die."

"It's just a line in a song, Merle."

"But as long as the song lives, so will the dreams that gave it life."

I nodded in agreement.

Merle Haggard died a little more than a year after we sang this song. It's not surprising that, on the night I heard he had passed, he came to me in a dream. I can't remember what he said, but he was singing, playing his guitar and making me feel that everything was all right. Merle was smiling.

FORGIVING YOU WAS EASY

Forgiving you was easy
But forgetting seems to take the longest time
I just keep thinking
And your memory is forever on my mind

You know I'll always love you
And I can't forget the days when you were
   mine
Forgiving you is easy
But forgetting seems to take the longest time

The bitter fruit of anger
Growing from the seeds of jealousy
Oh what a heartache
But I forgive the things you said to me

'Cause I believe forgiving
Is the only way that I'll find peace of mind
And forgiving you is easy
But forgetting seems to take the longest time

The years have passed so quickly
As once again fate steals a young man's
   dreams
Of all the golden years
And growing old together you and me

You asked me to forgive you
You said there was another on your mind
Forgiving you is easy
But forgetting seems to take the longest time

This is a young man's song written by middle-aged me. It came to me just a few years before I turned fifty. When it became a number one hit, a deejay asked if I was surprised. I wasn't. I said I wouldn't have written it if I didn't think it was a hit. I feel that way about all my songs.

I hope that doesn't sound conceited. But that's always been my mindset. I think I'm able to channel the feelings of the common man and common woman because I'm a common man. I don't try to second-guess feelings. I just try to let feelings flow through me. And I'm sure my feelings—especially those about love and loss—are about the same as most people's.

Take this business of forgiving and forgetting. The Good Book says forgive, and so we try. We know that holding on to hate corrodes the heart. But saying we forgive and actually doing it are two different deals.

In this song, I take on the life of a young guy who's been left high and dry. His girl is gone. She's found another, and though he claims he's forgiven her, I wonder if he can. It's one thing to forgive a woman; it's another to forgive fate. When circumstances conspire to rob you of happiness, how do you find peace?

"Just forget about her" is the old adage. But if he could, he would. If he really could forgive, then forgetting would follow. The problem—at least from where I sit—is that forgiving and forgetting are like leaves on the same branch of a tree. They fall to the ground in winter only to grow back in spring.

Ray Price and Merle Haggard have been big parts of my life and career. I miss them both.

THE WALL

I took on more than I could handle
I bit off more than I could chew
I hit the wall
I went off like a Roman candle
Burning everyone I knew
I hit the wall

And the wall came down
Crashing down
And there was not a sound

Half my life riding on a rocket
From one world to the next and on and on
I hit the wall
Taking things to make it make me better
Remembering things I never knew I knew
I hit the wall

And the wall came down
Roaring, crashing down
And there was not a sound

Let's talk about walls.

Walls separate. They divide us one from another. And even worse, they wall us off from ourselves.

"I hit the wall" is a strange expression. Who built the wall you hit? And what kept you from avoiding it? Rather than run into it, why didn't you climb over it?

Looking through an art book the other day, a painting caught my eye. A long single-story house was drawn with walls everywhere, some short, some tall, some close together. The walls were drawn helter-skelter. The design made no sense. A man was lost in one part of the house, his back against one wall, while a woman, looking to find him, faced an insurmountable wall of her own.

Felt like the human condition.

I like paintings because they're silent. I think of silent walls. When the wall collapses, it's eerily silent. Something's gone that you didn't know was there.

Humpty Dumpty sat on a wall and had a great fall. But we don't know why he was sitting there or why he fell. All we know is that all the king's horses and all the king's men couldn't put that sucker back together again.

If we find a way over or around or under the wall, we have a chance. But if we don't see the wall coming, we're toast.

Watch out for those walls.

Walls separate. They divide us one from another. And even worse, they wall us off from ourselves.

IS THE BETTER PART OVER?

Is the better part over?
Has a raging river turned into a stream?
Is the better part over?
Are we down to not quite saying what we mean?

And after thinking it over
Wouldn't you rather have the ending nice and clean
Where love remains in all the closing scenes?
If the better part's over

Why hang around
For an ending that's laden with sorrow?
We've both been around
We've both seen that movie before

And as much as I love you
I can't live while fearing tomorrow
If the better part's over
Then why should we try anymore?

I'm friends with a wide variety of individuals, from truck drivers to film directors to dog walkers to doctors of philosophy. One acquaintance specializes in psychology.

At age ninety, I'm not exactly a good candidate for traditional therapy. I'm not sure I've been a good candidate at any age. But when this guy talks about a nontraditional therapy based on storytelling, I get intrigued.

"What is it exactly?" I ask.

"It's called narrative therapy. It's based on the notion that how you tell your story actually changes your story."

"How can that be?" I ask. "The story you're telling has already happened."

"Yes, but you have choices in the way to tell an old story. And the choice you make impacts your present story."

"Give me an example," I say.

"I tell you that my childhood was marked by a mean father, and I've been suffering ever since. In telling that story, I continue my suffering. But if I tell you that my mean father taught me the pitfalls of being mean—and how I'm using his negative example to positive effect—I leave my suffering frame of mind. I'm reshaping my old story so my new story can be a happy one."

"So if, in a song, I ask the question 'Is the Better Part Over?', am I hurting or helping myself?"

"Asking questions always helps. Questioning implies curiosity, and curiosity leads to knowledge."

"How you tell your story actually changes your story."

RED HEADED STRANGER

They called it a concept album.

Maybe.

They said the title, *Red Headed Stranger,* applied to me. They said that I was, in fact, the red headed stranger.

Maybe.

To make the album, the label gave me a $60,000 advance because they were sure it'd cost me at least $40,000 to record it.

I recorded it for $2,000.

When I turned it in, the suits hated it. Said it sounded tinny and unfinished. Said the combination of old songs and new ones was confusing. Said it wouldn't sell.

I said, "Tough." My contract gave me creative control. I liked it the way it was. I thought music fans would feel the same.

They did. When it came out in 1975, it sold like hotcakes.

And whether I thought the handle of "Red Headed Stranger" fit me or not, it stuck. Folks call me that to this day. I'd rather just be called "Willie," but call me whatever you wanna. Just call me.

And whether
I thought
the handle of
"Red Headed
Stranger" fit
me or not, it
stuck. Folks
call me that
to this day.

If there's any concept to this album, it comes out of the title song that wasn't written by me, but by Edith Lindeman and Carl Stutz in 1953 for crooner Perry Como. Perry never got around to recording it, but Arthur "Guitar Boogie" Smith did. When I was deejaying at KCNC in Fort Worth in the mid-fifties, I'd play Boogie's version every day and dedicate it to my daughter Lana. I'd also sing it to her at night. It's a helluva song, a portrait about a cowpoke from Blue Rock, Montana, who loses his mind—he's "wild in his sorrow"—over the loss of his wife. Aimlessly, he rides his stallion through the countryside with his wife's horse trailing behind. When a wanton woman tries to steal the riderless horse, he kills her in cold blood.

For all the murderous drama, the song sings like a soothing lullaby. The contrast between tenderness and terror is captivating.

I ran with the story but took it in a few different directions. My concept for a suite of semi-connected songs was more fragmented than cohesive, but that was okay. If there are rules for storytelling, I never learned them.

The biggest surprise coming out of *Red Headed Stranger* was how the one song that only marginally fit into the concept, another song I didn't write—"Blue Eyes Crying in the Rain"—soared to the top of the charts.

Now let me see if I can stitch together my scattered thoughts about this strange album about a stranger who, after nearly fifty years, still lingers somewhere in the back of my mind.

TIME OF THE PREACHER

It was the time of the preacher
When the story began
And the choice of a lady
And the love of a man

I loved her so dearly
He went out of his mind
When she left him for someone
That she'd left behind

And he cried like a baby
And he screamed like a panther
In the middle of the night
And he saddled his pony
And he went for a ride

It was a time of the preacher
In the year of '01
Now the preaching is over
And the lesson's begun

I closed my eyes and pretended I was at a movie theater.

On the big screen I saw a character. In my reinvention of the red headed stranger, a minister is heading out into the great unknown because, for reasons unknown, he's lost his lady.

When I wrote the lyrics, I referred to this character as "he." Throughout the song, I keep using "he" except for one time. One of the label executives, who wasn't crazy about the song anyway, pointed out that in verse two I sing "I": "*I* loved her so dearly."

"You made a mistake, Willie," the record man said. "You meant to sing 'he.' You better go back and change it."

I considered his comment for a few seconds before saying, "I don't think I'll do that."

"Why not? You're being inconsistent. You're not that preacher. You're writing about the preacher."

"I guess in some ways I'm every character I write about. At least part of me is."

"It doesn't make sense to switch from 'he' to 'I.' Your fans won't understand."

"Maybe," I said, "but I'm guessing that my fans are smarter than you think."

My first three children: Lana, Susie, and Billy.

MEDLEY:
BLUE ROCK MONTANA /
RED HEADED STRANGER

He rode into Blue Rock, dusty and tired
And he got him a room for the night
He lay there in silence with too much on his
    mind
Still hoping that he was not right

But he found them that evening at a tavern in
    town
In a quiet little out-of-the-way place
And they smiled at each other when he walked
    through the door
And they died with their smiles on their faces
They died with a smile on their face

Don't boss him, don't cross him, he's wild in
    his sorrow
He's riding and hiding his pain
Don't fight him, don't spite him, just wait till
    tomorrow
Maybe he'll ride on again

Blue Rock doesn't exist. It's a made-up city mentioned in the original "Red Headed Stranger" song. I like the sound of the hamlet and, keeping a movie in mind, I see my man drifting all over the rugged state of Montana until his gut tells him to stop off in Blue Rock.

He gets a room in an old broken-down inn, hoping for the best but expecting the worst. He feels like he's following fate, and fate won't allow him to turn back.

Off the beaten road, he finds himself wandering into a tavern. Something tells him not to enter. Something else tells him he's got no choice. He has to go inside.

What are the chances that at the very moment our stranger walks through the door, his wife and her lover are munching on some pork and beans? What are the chances that he catches them glancing at each other with the look of love in both their eyes? What are the chances that he's able to restrain his rage, turn around, and leave them in peace?

There's no chance. No way for him not to do what his grief demands. Looking at the lovers, his head explodes. His gun explodes.

I don't need to describe the blood-soaked scene. You can see it for yourself.

WILLIE NELSON

RED HEADED STRANGER

R.H.S. Productions & Pangaea in association with Wrangler Jeans present
A Willie Nelson / Bill Wittliff Production of Red Headed Stranger
Starring WILLIE NELSON   MORGAN FAIRCHILD   R.G. ARMSTRONG
ROYAL DANO & KATHARINE ROSS as LAURIE   Produced by WILLIE NELSON & BILL WITTLIFF
Associate Producers DAVID ANDERSON   ETHEL VOSGITEL & BARRY FEY
Director of Photography NEIL ROACH   Original Music by WILLIE NELSON
Written & Directed by BILL WITTLIFF

An Alive Films Release

DENVER

The bright lights of Denver are shining like diamonds
Like ten thousand jewels in the sky
And it's nobody's business where you're going or where you come from
And you're judged by the look in your eye

She saw him that evening in a tavern in town
In a quiet little out-of-the-way place
And they smiled at each other as he walked through the door
And they danced with their smiles on their faces
And they danced with a smile on their face

Sometimes stories get so sad that they need to be spun in a different direction. That's how I was feeling about our stranger.

Maybe he skips Blue Rock altogether. Maybe he keeps moving on through Montana and moseys down through Wyoming into Colorado. When he gets to Denver, the world lights up. His heart brightens. If he's following fate, maybe fate isn't cruel; maybe fate is kind.

This time maybe fate leads him to a little café lit by candlelight. A man strums a guitar. The tables are empty except for one. She sits alone. It's as if she knew he'd come find her. More than surprised, she's serene. She realizes it's all meant to be.

When she left, she had her doubts. But she also felt free to explore something new. When that newness dissolved, so did her doubts. She wanted him back. And there was nothing she had to do to get him back. He'd find her.

And when he did, they would smile, and they would dance, and Denver would be a city of forgiveness, a city of forgotten love remembered, a city of starlit dreams and rekindled romance.

Rather than winding up in hell, the Red Headed Stranger has found heaven. And everyone lives happily ever after.

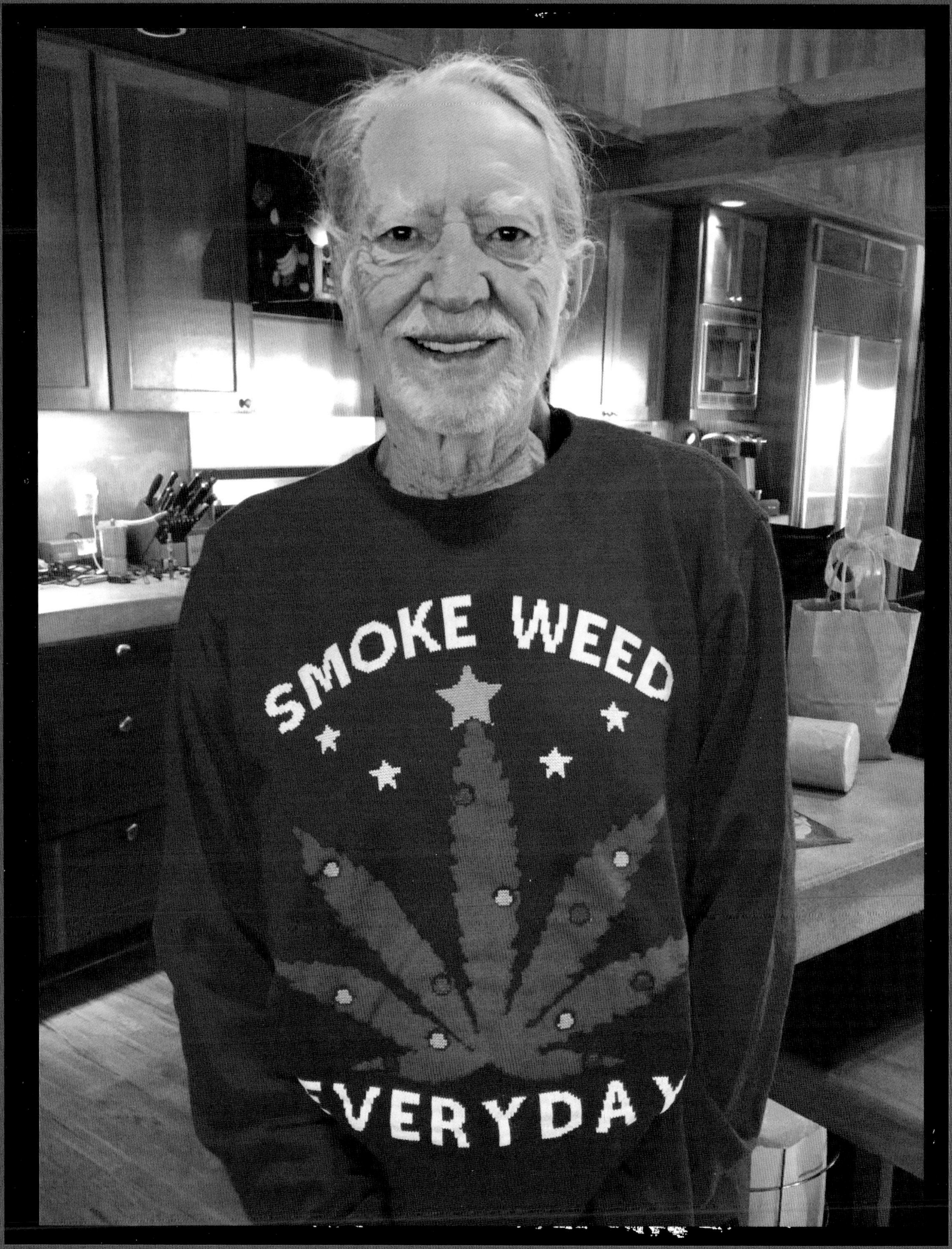
SMOKE WEED
EVERYDAY

CRAZY CHARACTERS

In writing about oddball folks I've met along the way, I don't see them as separate from me. I'm as oddball as it gets. Maybe that's why I appreciate my brothers and sisters who don't worry about looking and thinking like everyone else. I value individuality. I love uniqueness. And yes, I'm all for craziness if craziness means that in a crazy world you're determined to go your own way. I haven't gone my own way out of ego or spite or anger. I've gone the only way I could have gone without selling my soul to the devil.

To deal with this devilish condition on planet earth, craziness can be a pretty good strategy for survival. It's probably saved me from the so-called sanity of a society suffocating anyone and everything that can't be squeezed into little boxes. Breaking out of those boxes is not just the job of the artist. It's the job of everyone looking to find his, her, and their righteous place on the planet.

So here's to all of us, the crazy characters that keep life from turning into a dull grind. I say, the crazier the characters the better our chances of walking through life with happiness and hope.

PRETTY PAPER

Pretty paper, pretty ribbons of blue
Wrap your presents to your darling from you
Pretty pencils to write I love you
Pretty paper, pretty ribbons of blue

Crowded streets, busy feet, hustle by him
Downtown shoppers, Christmas is nigh
There he sits all alone on the sidewalk
Hoping that you won't pass him by

Should you stop? Better not, much too busy
You're in a hurry, my how time does fly
In the distance the ringing of laughter
And in the midst of the laughter he cries

Pretty paper, pretty ribbons of blue
Wrap your presents to your darling from you
Pretty pencils to write "I love you"
Pretty paper, pretty ribbons of blue

Family Christmas with Lukas, Annie, Micah, and Micah's wife, Alex.

I wrote this Christmas song in 1963 thinking I'd sing it. Fortunately, a better singer than me—Roy Orbison—turned it into a hit. I based the story on a legless man who sat on a wheeled cart in front of Leonard's Department Store in Fort Worth selling wrapping paper and ribbons. I'd seen him several times.

He fascinated me to where, beyond writing a tune, I fabricated a novel about whom he might be and how he happened to find himself rolling around a tough town like Fort Worth.

Both in the song and the novel, though, I eliminated one fact to save the sentiment of the story. Now, though, it's time to come clean.

It's true that the man worked diligently from his cart, crying out, "Pretty paper for sale!" It's also true that many shoppers, caught up in the holiday rush, ignored him. You couldn't help but feel sorry for the guy. However . . .

On one particular Saturday night I happened to catch a glimpse of him. It was cold and rainy. He did his best to cover his wares with a cloth but was having a hard time. I decided to help. I crossed the street and was just about to lend him a hand. Before I could reach him, though, a car pulled up. It was a baby blue, brand-new, top-of-the-line Cadillac. A woman was driving. She got out, gave the man a kiss on the cheek, and gathered up his merchandise. When I asked if she needed help in hauling him and his cart into the car, she shook her head. She was clearly in command. She lifted him up like he was light as a feather—and off they went.

A cynical observer standing next to me whispered, "Nice work if you can get it."

ALICE IN HULALAND

Alice in Hulaland
Building castles in the sand
Living life, ain't got no plan
Just loving the boys in the band

Alice in Hulaland
Painting daisies on her van
She's number one, their biggest fan
She loves the boys in the band

Alice in Hulaland
Come sit here on the front row
And get close to the sound
As close as you can

Are you there for the melody?
There for the lyrics?
Or just for the boys in the band?

Alice in Hulaland
Yellow bird, sitting on her hand
Singing to her, she understands
She loves the boys in the band

Alice in Hulaland
Come sit here on the front row
And get close to the sound
As close as you can
Are you there for the melody?
There for the lyrics?
Or just for the boys in the band?

Stan Cohen is an old friend of mine, a good-hearted guy who owns a T-shirt souvenir shop in Paia on Maui. I never asked him why he called the place Alice in Hulaland but presumed he was thinking of Lewis Carroll's classic novel about Alice in Wonderland.

I never read the book, but I knew it was about going down a rabbit hole. God knows I've gone down many a rabbit hole in my time. I loved the name of Stan's store and decided to use it as the title of a song. The challenge was painting a portrait of Alice.

Paia has a definite hippie vibe. That's why I love the place. And so why not make Alice a hippie? Paia is filled with music lovers, so why not make Alice a passionate music fan? Naturally, she'd have a van, and naturally, she'd want to paint flowers all over it.

I had seen many Alices at many festivals, picnics, and shows. They were free spirits. Some of them liked the boys in the band as much as the music that the boys were playing.

I wrote up the story and sent it to Buddy Cannon, who gave the music a surf-like Hawaiian flavor. During the *Django and Jimmie* session, I asked Merle what he thought of it. He listened to the lyrics and said, "I know Alice. I've known her for years."

"So you mind singing about her?" I asked.

"Hell no," said Merle. "I'd like it even more if she could be here watching us sing."

God knows I've gone down many a rabbit hole in my time.

MY HEART WAS A DANCER

My heart was a dancer
And though you don't need to know her name
She could turn on a nickel and give you back four cents in change

My heart was a dancer
She made her living on her toes
And what she ever saw in me
Only God in heaven will ever know

I used to sit at my table
Just me and whiskey all alone
Watching my heart dance
And each night I'd try to take her home

Others would try to show my heart
A better way to feel
My heart was a dancer
Oh heart, please don't be still

My heart was a dancer
I'd love to see her dancing now
Pretty and graceful
Still being just for me somehow

My heart was a dancer
Another lifetime ago
She was real for me
Before the others it was all just a show

The heart is a muscle, and I do my best to keep mine strong. But the heart is also a character with a mind all its own. A crazy character with a crazy mind. I'm not sure exactly what I had in mind when, not all that long ago, I wrote this song, but it's clear I got mixed up. I somehow turned my heart into a dancing woman.

The idea was to visualize a fantasy lady who danced through my dreams. Because I'm a man who has never stopped dreaming, there have been countless such ladies in countless dreams. There have even been a few in real life.

When the story fell out of me, though, I didn't give the woman a name. I could have called her Sophia or Roberta or Clara or Jane. I could have called her anything. Instead, I called the nameless lady "my heart." That felt right. Because in this fantasy, she turned into my heart and my heart turned into her.

As long as she was dancing, we mystically merged into one. But the moment I tried to possess her, she danced out of my dreams and disappeared into thin air. It made no sense. Why couldn't she see how much I wanted her? How much I loved her?

The "I" in the song could be any man. Men can't stop fantasizing. Maybe that's a bad thing since fantasies aren't real. But if you're a songwriter, it's a good thing. Not only do fantasies make for good songs, but there's an endless supply of them. They never stop haunting you, even (and especially) in old age.

A LEAR AND A LIMO

I don't want it all, just a little
I'll give it all back when I'm through
'Cause life don't owe me a living
But a Lear and limo will do

I traveled the world
Till I'm blue in the face
And the blues ain't nothing new

Money and fame's
Not an amateur's game
And baby, neither are you

'Cause I don't want it all, just a little,
I'll give it all back when I'm through
I just want to break even or else I'll be
    leaving
It all to someone like you

Mickey Raphael is my harmonica man. He's a master of that instrument and one of my musical mainstays. Mickey also helped put together this book of songs.

I met Mickey at a jam session in Dallas through University of Texas football coach Darrell Royal, a good friend and big-time music fan. Darrell had me and Charley Pride trading licks. When Mickey joined in, I saw his future before he did. When he joined my band, he was twenty, our youngest member. Now, at seventy, he's our oldest member after me.

Mickey and I wrote this little ditty during a time he calls "the decadent period." By that he means that I owned a Learjet. It was 1978. He and I had places in Malibu and, although the rest of the band didn't like flying, we loved it. We flew back to Southern California whenever our schedule allowed. We were usually the only two passengers. With nothing to do except reflect on the good life, we started scribbling down a few thoughts.

I'm not sure who inserted the part about the woman who may or may not be a positive part of the good life, but I have a feeling it was me. Not that Mickey isn't a ladies' man. He just may (or may not) have a less complicated relationship with the fairer sex than me.

BAD BREATH

Don't ever complain about nothing
Before we can walk we all gotta crawl
"Halitosis" is a word I never could spell
But bad breath is better than no breath at all

It's okay to say "hello" to me
But don't get too near if you don't wanna fall
And don't think you'll love me if my breath
    melts the wall
'Cause bad breath is better than no breath
    at all

I've been a-puffin' on this and a-suckin' on that
I got feeling a thousand feet tall
The closer we get you'll have to agree
That bad breath is better than no breath at all

I been talking to the man in the mirror
And he smells like his diet is rotgut alcohol
But it's better I guess than starving to death
And bad breath is better than no breath at all

A song that only an elderly citizen would have the guts to write.

In my twenties and thirties, even in my sixties or seventies, I'm not sure I'd want to sing about some old guy with nasty breath.

Don't presume the old guy is me. My wife is always slipping me a mint when I need one.

Don't presume the old guy isn't me. Sometimes my wife isn't around when a mint is a must.

But you *can* presume this: I'm one hundred percent behind the line that says, "Bad breath is better than no breath."

Various Eastern religions have been focusing on breath since time immemorial. We Westerners tend to take breath for granted. We overlook its spiritual property.

Consciousness of breath is cosmic. We're breathed by a force—call that what you will—that's linked to time eternal.

I don't know if I'll ever get to the point where I can feel gratitude for *every* breath I take, but it's something to aim for. Every breath as a gift. Every breath as a reminder to stay rooted in present time.

The gurus say meditate on your breath.

Breathe in the good stuff like love. Breathe out the bad stuff like bitterness.

And while you're breathing, who cares if your breath smells like lilacs or stinks of garlic?

First & Goal

He was born to the game
call it football by name -
or call it life call it love -
call it soul -
And he came here to win
he's done it time and again -
cause every mornin' it's first & goal

to " the Coach Royal "

Jan 2 - 72 -

Willie Nelson

Willie was our guest at the Cotton Bowl
game Jan 1 1972. He left this for Darrell.

SO YOU THINK YOU'RE A COWBOY

So you think you're a cowboy but you're only a kid
With a mind to do everything wrong
And it starts to get smoother when the circle begins
But by the time that you get there it's gone

So you think you're a winner but you're losing again
The cards have already been dealt
And the hand that you're holding means nothing at all
Just knowing is all that is there

So you think you're a cowboy but you're only a kid
With a mind to do everything wrong
And it starts to get smoother when the circle begins
But by the time that you get there it's gone

So your life is finding the best that you can
Tomorrow is not right or wrong
And don't wait for tomorrow to bring you your dreams
'Cause by the time that they get there they're gone

Wild Bill Elliott. Lash LaRue. Tex Ritter. Whip Wilson. Hopalong Cassidy. These were my first and forever heroes, cowboy film stars galloping across the movie screens of the little towns, West and Hillsboro, close to my Abbott home. I idolized them for three reasons: They shot straight; they won the hearts of beautiful women; and, especially in the case of Gene Autry and Roy Rogers, they played guitar and sang pretty.

When Hank Cochran and I wrote this song back in the day, I went back to even earlier days when I snuck in the side door and sat through a Saturday matinee, mesmerized by the shoot-'em-ups. I was a cowboy in mind only. I knew nothing about real-life cowboys. Knew nothing about the cold world and the crooked paths that awaited me.

The song came out in 1980 on the soundtrack for *Honeysuckle Rose*. Instead of playing a cowboy, I played a country singer (who probably, like most country singers, wanted to be a cowboy). I didn't sing it in the film. Emmylou Harris did. She sang it in front of a live audience, lending it a female perspective. I loved her interpretation. Women have more of a clear-eyed understanding of the foolishness of young boys than us men.

Men have a tough time getting over their cowboy fantasies. Even when we know better, in the back of our heads we still think one day we'll strike out for new territory and, in the freedom of the Wild West that never was, become who we were never meant to be.

SUPERMAN

Too many pain pills too much pot
Trying to be something that I'm not
Superman, Superman
Trying to do more than I can
I got a little out of hand
I ain't Superman

Well I blew my throat and I blew my tour
I wound up sipping on soup du jour
I wasn't Superman, I wasn't Superman
I'm trying to do more than I can
I got a little out of hand
I wasn't Superman

Well, the doctor said, "Son, it's a crying shame
But you ain't Clark Kent and I ain't Lois Lane"
You ain't Superman, you ain't Superman
Trying to do more than you can
Got a little out of hand
You ain't Superman

And when I die put it on my stone
God said, "Sucker, get your bad ass home
You wasn't Superman"

I wasn't Superman
Trying to do more than I can
I got a little out of hand
I wasn't Superman

Around 2009, my lungs weren't pumping properly. The doctor called it pneumonia and told me to take a break for a couple of months.

That meant no touring and no weed. Given that performing and smoking are among my favorite things, kicking back wasn't easy. It was during this period that I started thinking thoughts like, "I had all my medication and it's half-past ten . . . I'm just sitting around waiting for something to kick in."

Sounded like the inspiration for a song that I finished up in no time flat. It's nothing more than a reminder to myself that, even though I love getting high, I can't put on a cape and fly.

As fate would have it, in 2010 I was all healed up and in Amsterdam, a city famous for legal pot. We were playing a club called Melkweg when who should turn up but my friend Snoop Dogg, a brother who is not only a great writer but also a fellow weed lover. Snoop got onstage and sang the hell out of "Superman" with me. When it was time for Mickey Raphael to take a solo, a highlight of the song, Snoop said, "Blow, Slick Mick, blow!"

Snoop's a dynamite duet partner, and we had so much fun we decided to do it live on the Dave Letterman show. We had another blast.

When Snoop was interviewed about our friendship, he said something I liked hearing. "There's only one man I've met who smoked me under the table," he said, "and he goes by the name of Willie Hugh Nelson."

GHOST

The silence is unusually loud tonight
The strange sound of nothing fills my ears
Then night rushes in like a crowd of nights
And the ghost of our old love appears

This strange world of darkness that comes with the night
Grows darker when it walks my way
And it laughs while I listen for the breaking of day
And the ghost of our old love goes away

Art denies death.

Some folks are scared of ghosts. I'm not. Others are haunted by them. That's me. It's nearly impossible to love music and not feel the ghostly presence of spirits long gone. Whether it's Jack Teagarden or Bob Wills, Hoagy Carmichael or Ernest Tubb, Django Reinhardt or Frank Sinatra, armies of artists have flat-out refused to surrender to obsolescence. Their art denies death. They're still playing for us, writing for us, and singing to us.

I hear them both in my daydreams and my night dreams. When I play, write, and sing, I feel these spirits playing, writing, and singing along with me. I don't have to conjure them up. They're already there, part of me, part of you, part of the world of sound where time never stops and melodies linger forever.

Like music, old lovers can haunt us as well. The memories may be bittersweet, the relationships may not have survived, but the ghosts of those loves have a way of hanging around.

I was young when I wrote this song—not much older than thirty—and it surprises me how, during those early days, my imagination was visited by ghosts. I was probably channeling another soul whose name I never knew and whose story, although not mine, crept into my head and wouldn't leave until it came out as a song.

I'M STILL HERE

Two old men are sitting on a bench. Both are frail. They could be on the coast of Maine or the Mississippi Gulf. The sun is shining. Birds are chirping. Flowers are blooming. The world is peaceful. They've known each other forever. They've heard each other's stories so often there's nothing more to say. They're content just to watch the young women jogging along the trail right there in front of them.

Finally, one says to the other, "I'm going to ask something I've never asked you before."

"Ask."

"Are you afraid of dying?"

Several seconds of silence.

Finally, he answers with a shrug.

"That means no, you're not afraid?"

"That means I don't like the question."

"But you think about it, don't you?"

"When it comes to stupid questions like that, I only think of one thing."

"What one thing?"

"I'm still here."

I'M STILL HERE

When I come home at night somehow I know
    beyond a doubt
That my heart can't stand the loneliness that
    lives within my house
But daylight always comes before my heart
    gives up the fight
And I'm still here to cry again another night

I'm still here and love you more and more each
    day
Can't understand why either lies or memories
    don't fade away
But the memories keep coming and the end is
    not in sight
And I'm still here to cry again another night

I know I must have given up a hundred times
    before
But this stubborn heart of mine keeps right on
    coming back for more
There's bound to be a limit to the pain a heart
    can stand
But it won't stop until I've cried again—and
    again

Whenever I'm called stubborn, I can't argue. I can be stubborn as hell. Maybe that's why I'm still here. I'm too stubborn to be anywhere else.

For the life of me, I can't remember exactly when or why I wrote this song. From the sound of it, it had to be the sixties when I was cutting demos left and right. It's probably one of those demos that never made it onto a real album, not because I didn't like it, but because sometimes a song will fall in the cracks.

I have a feeling the title came to me first. It stuck. I still like the sound of saying, "I'm still here." I'm partial to short affirmative sentences. They tend to make me stand up straight. Might be close to seventy years since I wrote this thing, but, more than ever, I'm still pinching myself and saying, "I'm still here."

One philosopher said, "I think, therefore I am."

I'd have to say, "I sing, therefore I am."

I could say, "I write, therefore I am," but that's not true. I write my songs for me to sing. They don't really come to life until I sing them.

Naturally, I'm pleased when other singers pay me the compliment of covering my songs. But that's whipped cream on top of the cake. I bake the cake for me to eat. I can eat it without the whipped cream on top, though the whipped cream adds to the treat.

I think I'm still here because I like baking cakes. I have a knack for adding ingredients that deliver an aftertaste—sweet or sour—that you might not expect.

I'd give you the recipe, except there isn't any.

A guitar pull is an old Southern tradition. Bobby Bare, Kris Kristofferson, Harlan Howard, me, and Billy Walker took our turns strumming a tune on our guitars.

LAST MAN STANDING

I don't wanna be the last man standing
But wait a minute maybe I do
If you don't mind I'll start a new line
And decide after thinking it through

Go on in front if you're in such a hurry
Like hell ain't waiting for you
I don't wanna be the last man standing
On second thought maybe I do

It's getting hard to watch my pals check out
Cuts like a worn-out knife
One thing I learned about running the road
Is forever don't apply to life

Waylon and Ray and Merle and old Harlan
Lived just as fast as me
I still got a lotta good friends left
And I wonder who the next will be

Maybe we'll all meet again on the other side
We'll pick and sing and load up the buses and ride
I don't wanna be the last man standing
But on second thought maybe I do

If Bette Davis hadn't already said "old age isn't for sissies," I might have used that line for a song.

If you make it into your eighties, you can't help but think about death. Even if you follow the noble creed of one-day-at-a-time, you're forced to face the reality that many of your cronies have run out of days.

You can't help but wonder why you, who've lived as wild a life as your buddies, continue to live while they've moved on to glory.

They call it glory for a good reason. This new life that awaits us sounds exciting. What new form will we take? What new freedom will we enjoy? This present incarnation is fine but far from easy. The warring elements that make up mankind and womankind have a tough time finding peace.

At the same time, I don't mind hanging out a little longer in this land of the living. Can't say I'm all that anxious to move on.

Death is a deadly subject. To take off the edge, it helps to write an up-tempo song, a song with a vibe so happy that maybe for a minute I can forget the meaning of the message.

STILL NOT DEAD

I woke up still not dead again today
The internet said I had passed away
If I died, I wasn't dead to stay
I woke up still not dead again today

Well, I woke up still not dead again today
The gardener did not find me that a way
You can't believe a word that people say
And I woke up still not dead again today

I run up and down the road making music as I go
They say my pace would kill a normal man
But I've never been accused of being normal anyway
And I woke up still not dead again today

I woke up still not dead again today
The news said I was gone, to my dismay
Don't bury me, I've got a show to play
And I woke up still not dead again today

Last night I had a dream that I died twice yesterday
But I woke up still not dead again today

I have an iPhone, but that's about it. I don't do social media. I'm not sure I even understand social media. All I know is that there's a lot of nasty chatter out there. Thousands of folks are getting into fixes for posting things that don't need posting.

Yet hard as I try to avoid the pitfalls of modern technology, I can't. Like the air we breathe, the internet is everywhere. It's beautiful to have infinite information at our fingertips, but the price we pay is the meanness of misinformation.

So what happens to a man like me when he wakes up to learn that his obituary has been posted and he's presently being written about in the past tense?

Well, my first reaction is to pinch myself and make sure it isn't true. Once I establish the fact that, for better or worse, I'm still a living, breathing guitar picker, I better pick up my guitar and figure out how I feel about folks calling me dead.

What I figure out is that I'm grateful.

Bless the naysayers for giving me a whole new subject to explore. Fact is, I dedicate this living song to all those who are dead certain that I stopped living some time ago.

I'm still a living, breathing guitar picker.

FOLLOWING ME AROUND

She always follows me from town to town
At least her memories following me around
And whenever I clear my mind so she can see
I feel her love come rushing into me

I know that I will never be alone
It looks as though her memory's found a
    home
And I know my love will always stay in
    bounds
With her memory always following me
    around

And I know my love will always stay in
    bounds
With her memory always following me
    around
Following me around following me around
With her memory always following me
    around

When I sang this song for producer Felton Jarvis sometime in the sixties, he thought it could use a slightly Latin tinge.

I liked the idea; I love Spanish guitars and mariachi trumpets. Even before Felton heard it, the song had been chasing me for quite some time.

The fact that a song followed me around was nothing new. A story doesn't always arrive in completed form. Ideas float in and out of my mind. They can be like butterflies. They're never still for long. I'll catch a word here or a phrase there. And then I'll forget, only to remember while I'm sipping my coffee or brushing my teeth.

To be followed by a thought or memory can be an annoyance or a blessing. The annoyance is when the thought is painful and the memory dark—when the dark pain won't leave me alone; when I feel like I'll do anything to escape the prison of the past. The blessing is when I push past the dark pain into the present—when I use the emotion and turn it into a story that can be sung by me, or by anyone, looking to follow the path flooded with light.

I believe in spiritual forces that calm and center our restless souls. I believe in healers and healing. But I'm not sure that hurt hearts ever heal completely. Hurt follows us around forever. That's why sad songs stay with us. They tell the truth.

SOMETHING YOU GET THROUGH

When you lose the one you love
You think your world has ended
You think your world will be a waste of life
Without them in it

You feel there's no way to go on
Life is just a sad, sad song
But love is bigger than us all
The end is not the end at all

It's not something you get over
But it's something you get through
It's not ours to be taken
It's just a thing we get to do

Life goes on and on
And when it's gone
It lives in someone new

It's not something you get over
But it's something you get through

I don't believe in endings.
I believe in changes.

A half century had passed since I penned "Following Me Around." I was on the bus trying to comfort a friend who had just lost his wife. I said, "It isn't something you ever get over. It's more like something you get through." My cowriter Buddy Canon was with us and heard what I said. "That's a song," he suggested. Buddy was right: My best hope was to work out my emotions in song.

I tried to be honest. Losing a loved one is an open wound that stays open. The pain is permanent. To pretend otherwise only prolongs the pain and makes you more miserable. I can attest to that.

I can also say that I don't believe in endings. I believe in changes. I can't fully understand love, but I do know that love was here yesterday, love is here today, and love will be here tomorrow. Love exists outside of time.

At some point sadness stops. For that matter, so does happiness. They're just fleeting feelings. While they're with us, those feelings are strong. Yet they don't stay forever. Love does.

Love can't be defeated. In my view, we can only defeat ourselves by denying the love that exists all around us. It's hard—it may even seem impossible—to find hope amid despair, but it's something I feel the need to sing about. It's my own way of consoling someone, especially myself, when grief feels indelible. Some grief you never get over, but, leaning on love, you can get through it.

NOBODY SAID IT WAS GOING TO BE EASY

Nobody said it was going to be easy
It's only as hard as it seems
But lately it's harder than usual
Am I dreaming impossible dreams?

Will you love me forever, I don't even know
And I don't really care anymore
Nobody said it was going to be easy
It never was easy before

In 1983, Kris Kristofferson and I costarred in a movie written by my friend Bud Shrake, *Songwriter*. We needed a song to be sung by Melinda Dillon, who played my wife. Mickey Raphael, who also had a role in the film, joked, "Nobody said it was going to be easy being Willie's wife."

I liked the phrase. It fit my character just fine.

Mickey and I kicked around the idea. He said that he looked up to me as a mentor, brother, and father figure. I was glad to hear it. But he also was candid enough to admit that working in the Willie world wasn't going to be easy.

That's when we put our heads together and wrote the song.

And it *was* easy!

"Easy is as easy does" is something we've heard all our lives. But when you break it down, what does it mean? Not exactly sure. All I can say is that when I view a task as difficult, or even impossible, I feel pressure. I get to feeling anxious. But if I remember that no one promised me that anything is going to be easy, I can ease into a whole different attitude. I can ease into thinking that easy is a state of mind. I can convince myself since nothing is easy, maybe everything is easy. How do you accomplish that? By rolling with the punches, you just take it easy.

READY TO ROAR

Get down the fiddle and break out the bow
Take off the gloves and throw down the hoe
Worked hard all week my back is sore
It's Friday night and I'm ready to roar

Ready to roar, ready to roar
It's five o'clock and I'm out that door
I'm hot and dusty, I'm tired and wore
But it's Friday night and I'm ready to roar

I've been picking this up and putting that
   down
Tired of my boss bossing me around
Changing my clothes going into town
Find a little love and drink a little down

Ready to roar, ready to roar
It's five o'clock and I'm out that door
I'm hot and dusty, I'm tired and wore
But it's Friday night and I'm ready to roar

Well, I picked up a lid from a friend of mine
And the man picked me up now I'm doing
   time
But I'll get out tomorrow and if you see my
   friend
Tell him meet me at the bar and we can try
   that again

He might not know me 'cause I'm low-class
Tell him I'm the one with his head up his ass

Ready to roar, ready to roar
It's five o'clock and I'm out that door
I'm hot and dusty, I'm tired and wore
But it's Friday night and I'm ready to roar

My costars from the movie *Songwriter*, Kris Kristofferson and Lesley Ann Warren.

Sometimes you can't take it easy; sometimes you can't stand still or stop from running.

Working men and working women know what I'm talking about. The job is tedious, the hours brutal, the weekday long. You watch the clock until it looks like the second hand has stopped. You think it's already Thursday when it turns out to be Tuesday. Way back in 1947, T-Bone Walker, the great Texas bluesman, wrote "Call It Stormy Monday (But Tuesday Is Just as Bad)." He said the "eagle flies on Friday," meaning Friday is payday, and Saturday is playday.

I'm not sure I was thinking of T-Bone when, seventy years after his let-loose blues hit the airwaves, I wrote my own version of Thank-God-It's-Friday. I was in my mid-eighties and still feeling for the folks I'd been around my whole life, people on the nine-to-five who needed relief from the grueling grind.

In my little ditty, I spiced up the story with a dope buy gone bad, but not too bad. My man gets sprung from the slammer in time to go back to being bad.

Some songs don't have to do anything but make you feel good. And the best of those songs make you feel good about feeling bad.

ALWAYS NOW

It's always now
And nothing ever goes away
Everything is here to stay
And it's always now

It's always now
There never was a used to be
Everything is still with me
And it's always now

So brace your heart
Save yourself some sanity
It's more than just a memory
And it's always now

And here's your part
Sing it like a melody
There's really only you and me
And it's always now

There's really only you and me
And it's always now

A common piece of wisdom is "be here now." I like that because it reminds me to get our ass out of the past, stop thinking about the future, and stay planted in the present.

Whether we heed this direction to "be here now" doesn't really matter. We have no choice. The "now" is all we got.

Our minds wander. We go tripping off in different directions. But the wandering and tripping is part of our now. I don't judge the wandering and the tripping. I just call it present moment wandering and tripping.

We can handle the now any way we want. In the now, we can be calm or agitated. In the now, we can be reflective or regretful. It's up to us.

For my part, it's simple: I'm just grateful that, in the now, I'm still breathing.

Yet even when the day arrives that I stop breathing, the now will stay. I'll still be in the now, because the now, like love, is forever. It doesn't expand or contract. Its cosmic presence is permanent.

As I write these words, I write them in the now. When I read them later, I'll also be in the now. And the same goes for you when you read them. You'll be in the now.

Now—three little letters—is a beautiful word. And a beautiful way to live life.

My second wife, the super-talented Shirley Collie.

TOUGHER *than* LEATHER

"Damn right it's a concept album," Paul English told me when I put out *Tougher Than Leather* in 1983.

"What's the concept?" I asked.

"Look at the cover, Willie."

The cover was a picture of one of Paul's hand-tooled saddles with matching roses and elaborate vines. Paul was a gifted leather tooler.

"When I look at the cover," I said, "I see your saddle with my face stuck in the middle."

"You just called out the concept. You're tougher than leather and all these songs prove it."

All that the album proved was that I could still write songs. Period. If that shows toughness, well, I'll take it.

It had been eight years since the release of *Red Headed Stranger,* an album that contained mainly original songs. In its aftermath, I'd recorded *Stardust*, my covers of the American songbook, plus an album where I sang Kris Kristofferson songs, followed by other records where I covered tunes from various genres.

So I figured it was time for original material. That's how *Tougher Than Leather* was born. If there's a story that connects the songs in *Tougher Than Leather,* it's a subtle one, even an abstract one. It's the story of a human being—or many human beings—trying to figure out fate, a story so old that when it's told again, it feels new.

MY LOVE FOR THE ROSE

Was it something I did, Lord, a lifetime ago?
Am I just now repaying a debt that I owe?
Justice, sweet justice, you travel so slow
But you can't change my love for the rose

Family, friends, and fans send me jokes and quotes all the time.

I'm glad to get them. I'm always open to a new laugh or a little piece of wisdom. Got a cool quote just the other day. I was told it's from the Cuban American playwright María Irene Fornés: "Being an artist you have to abandon any notion of things making sense."

I like hearing that because when I strung together the songs that comprise *Tougher Than Leather*, I wasn't looking to make sense as much as I was looking to make music. I wanted to set a scene and sustain a mood.

It all began with a picture in my head of a red rose. Where that rose would take me I didn't know.

Brother Paul.

CHANGING SKIES

There's a bird in the sky
Flying high, flying high
To a place from a place
Changing skies, changing skies

There are clouds in the sky
Clouds of fear and despair
But love like ours never dies
Changing skies, changing skies

Little bird, have you heard
Freedom lies, freedom lies
But love like ours never dies
Just changing skies, changing skies

What does the rose have to do with a bird?

Not sure. All I can tell you is that a bird flew in the picture. High in the sky, the bird felt like freedom to me. How do birds make it through lightning and thunder and still survive? How do they read the changing skies?

I'm not a weatherman. I don't know if there's sunshine or hail ahead. All I can say is that the sky, like the ocean, excites my imagination. The vastness, the endless possibilities, the stories within stories within stories make me wonder where this bird is going to take me and what I'm going to see.

Life on the ranch keeps me grounded.

TOUGHER THAN LEATHER

He was Tougher Than Leather
And he didn't care whether
The sun shined or not

When a young kid from Cow Town
Wanted a showdown
He was careless or just maybe forgot

But he died in the gunfight
Blinded by sunlight
Never draw when you're facing the sun

And old Tougher Than Leather
Just carved one more notch on his gun
And when he turned to go

The beautiful maiden knelt down
Where her dead sweetheart lay
And on his breast placed a rose
While the townspeople stared in dismay

And old Tougher Than Leather
Should've known better
But he picked up the rose in his hand

And the townspeople froze
When his hands crushed the rose
And the rose petals fell in the sand

And old Tougher Than Leather
Was a full-time go-getter
The grass never grew beneath his feet

From one town to another
He would ride like the wind
But his mind kept going back to the street

Where a young cowboy died
And a young maiden cried
And rose petals fell in the sand

And his heart had been softened
By the beautiful maid
And he knew he must see her again

Well, he went back to the town
Where it all had come down
And he searched but his search was in vain

He had wanted to find her
And say he was sorry
For causing her heart so much pain

But one night he died from a poison inside
Brought on by the wrong he had done
And old Tougher Than Leather
Had carved his last notch on his gun

Well, he was buried in Cow Town
Along about sundown
Looking good in his new store-bought clothes

When the young maiden came over
And knelt down beside him
And on his lapel placed a rose

There's a bird in the sky
Flying high, flying high
To a place from a place
Changing skies, changing skies

This title song is way longer than anything else I've written.

That's because the story demanded it. The story hearkens back to my boyhood when my mind was captured by cowboys and gunfights and the women they loved and lost. I set things up in Fort Worth, the toughest town I knew as a youth. Fort Worth was where the Wild West began.

Because I'm not a paint-by-numbers storyteller, I didn't even bother to give the bad guy a name. It was enough to call him by the title of the song.

Tougher Than Leather surprised me. So did the appearance of the rose. My love for the rose must have been responsible for it playing such a big part in this little play. What kind of villain destroys the sweet symbol of the love a woman holds for the man he's just murdered?

But then the brute takes another route. There he is, heading back to the scene of the crime, his heart filled with remorse. Who would have guessed? By then, though, it was too late. Toxicity had trumped his newfound tenderness. Tougher Than Leather was a goner. Tougher Than Leather wasn't all that tough.

But the rose—that precious rose—had to return. And when it does, it returns in the form of forgiveness.

I was stunned by the act of mercy performed by the maiden who miraculously turns vengeance into grace.

Like the sky, people are always changing.

LITTLE OLD FASHIONED KARMA

There's just a little old fashioned karma
    coming down
Just a little old fashioned justice going round

A little bit of sowing and a little bit of reaping
A little bit of laughing and a little bit of
    weeping

Just a little old fashioned karma coming down
Coming down coming down
Just a little old fashioned karma coming down

It really ain't hard to understand
If you're gonna dance you gotta pay the band
It's just a little old fashioned karma coming
    down

If you grew up in Texas, you better play football.

My earliest example of good karma concerned my grandmother Mama Nelson. When her husband Daddy Nelson died in 1939 at age fifty-six, she and my big sister Bobbie were right to panic. Only six, I was too young to understand the implications. Because Mama Nelson had neither money nor means, social workers wanted to put me and Bobbie in separate foster homes. Daddy Nelson, the town blacksmith, had been the sole breadwinner. But Mama Nelson had the heart of a lioness and wouldn't let the state separate us. The citizenry of Abbott rallied around her. They sent their kids to her for music lessons. Farmers let her—along with me and Sister—work their fields. We ate the vegetables from the garden. Meals were sparse but we never starved.

Then karma kicked in. Good old-fashioned karma. Mama Nelson had spread such goodwill throughout her life that goodwill came smiling back her way. When our local school needed a cook for the cafeteria—a coveted job because it meant bringing home leftover food every night—the principal reached out to my grandmother.

Some call it good fortune. But Mama Nelson said it best:

"You get what you give."

SOMEWHERE IN TEXAS
(PART I)

Somewhere in Texas
A young cowboy dreams
Of the days when the buffalo roamed

And he wished he had lived then
'Cause he knew that he could have been
The best cowboy the world had ever known

He went dancing that night
With a San Antone rose
The one he would marry someday

To the music of Bob Wills
And polkas and waltzes
While beautiful time passed away

The sky clouds up, yet a ray of sunshine comes through. The bird is still flying high and suddenly a new story comes into view.

This one feels happy, at least from the start, and I relate to the scene. It's another kid from Texas, not unlike me, raised on fresh corn and beans.

I interrupt the story—but only briefly—to do a slick sleight of hand. I don't cheat at cards, but I guess you could call it cheating because on this concept album I stick in a song written way before the concept came to mind. I go back twelve years to *Yesterday's Wine*, my first concept album, and redo "Summer of Roses" just because *Tougher Than Leather* can always use another bunch of roses.

After this brief interlude, we go back to the boy who fell in love with an unnamed sweetheart from San Antonio to the music of a country singer named Bob Wills, one of my childhood heroes.

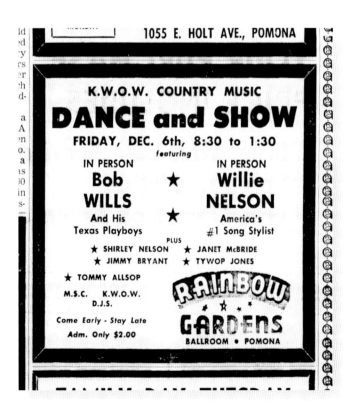

SOMEWHERE IN TEXAS (PART II) / MY LOVE FOR THE ROSE

Going home in this pickup
Not knowing this stickup
Was in progress on the same side of town

By a man in a truck
The same kind he was driving
Bad karma was soon coming down

Before the store owner died
He had tried to describe
The man who had shot him that day

And he described to a letter
The innocent cowboy
So they tried him and sent him away

Was it something I did, Lord, a lifetime ago?
Am I just now repaying a debt that I owe?
Justice, sweet justice, you travel so slow
But you can't change my love for the rose

They say the law of karma is absolute and that ultimately justice will prevail.

But when?

And where?

In this lifetime?

Or do we have to wait for another?

The promise of the rose is that love lives forever. But what about the expression that says, "The bloom is off the rose"? The petals fall. Its fragrance turns foul.

Fate feels like hate. Hope turns to horror.

And our hero is trapped in a story that he doesn't know how to get out of.

What's to become of him?

The bird is still flying, the sky is still changing, but something is wrong.

Terribly wrong.

"No, you can't drive, Lukas."

THE CONVICT AND THE ROSE / CHANGING SKIES

Within my prison cell so dreary
I sit alone with aching heart
I'm dreaming of my little darling
From her forever I must part

The rose she sent me as a token
She sent it just to light my gloom
And tell me that her heart is broken
And cheer me before I meet my doom

The judge would not believe my story
The jury said I'd have to pay
And with the rose in all its glory
Not guilty was all that I could say

Goodbye, sweetheart, for in the morning
To meet my maker I must go
And when I die at daylight's dawning
Against my heart they'll find this rose

There's a bird in the sky
Flying high, flying high
To a place from a place
Changing skies, changing skies

There are clouds in the sky
Clouds of fear and despair
But love like ours never dies
Changing skies, changing skies

Little bird, have you heard
Freedom lies, freedom lies
But love like ours never dies
Just changing skies, changing skies

Performing with members of my Family, Paul English, Bee Spears, and Mickey Raphael.

We're back to the blues.

As B.B. King said, "The blues is the bottom line."

For all this talk of good karma and mystical roses, shit happens. In the real world, too many times the innocent are found guilty and the guilty go free.

So the question becomes: What is freedom? Until heaven is created on earth, which I personally don't see happening any time soon, half the world remains in some form of bondage.

Earthbound freedom can be seen as a lie. To be truly free is to live in the otherworldly land of pure love, a land of undying dreams.

Down here, the blues keeps playing. The blues doesn't disappear. But up there, who knows?

I AM THE FOREST

I'll always be with you for as long as you please
For I am the forest but you are the trees

I'm empty without you so come grow within me
For I am the forest and you are the trees

And the heavens need romance so love never dies
You'll be the stars, dear, and I'll be the sky

And should any of this find us, let them all be forewarned
That you are the thunder and I am the storm

And I'll always be with you for as long as you please
For I am the forest and you are the trees

Henry David Thoreau was a helluva guy. In the summer of 1845, he retreated from the world to the wilds of Walden Pond to be close to nature. "I went to the woods," he wrote, "because I wished to live deliberately, to front only the essential facts of life, and see if I could not learn what it had to teach, and not, when I came to die, discover that I had not lived."

They called him and some of his friends "transcendentalists," because they wanted to transcend into new ways of thinking. One way of thinking was seeing creation as all one thing. You, me, the trees, the bees, the bears, the waterfalls, the rocks and stones and even the Spanish rose that grows in Harlem are all connected.

Connect to the star. Connect to the changing sky. Connect to the spirit that bubbles up inside us when we catch a glimpse of a rainbow. Realize we are that rainbow.

Transcend from thinking small to thinking big. Transcend from thinking itself. Transcend to accepting. Transcend to knowing that if you are me and I am you and we are all one thing, everything is everything and everything is just fine.

One way of thinking was seeing creation as all one thing.

NOBODY SLIDES, MY FRIEND

Nobody slides, my friend
It's a truth on which
You can depend

If you're living a lie
It will eat you alive
And nobody slides, my friend

Nobody slides, my friend
You can try it
But you'll never win

You can scream, you can shout
But it all evens out
And nobody slides, my friend

Nobody slides, my friend
Listen, I'll say it again

You can run, you can hide
But it's still waiting inside
And nobody slides, my friend

When it comes to stories, especially mine, take 'em or leave 'em. Some are cautionary tales, some are fairy tales, some are tall tales, and some, like the sound of a chirping bird, can be just as easily ignored as enjoyed.

If you ask me about the morals to any of my stories, I'd probably say there aren't any. But I'd be lying. I'd only say that because I don't like the sound of saying, "This story has a moral" or "This story has a message." That makes me sound like a cranky schoolteacher who takes himself too seriously.

But whether I like it or not, I have convictions that come out when I write. Here's one that I'm sticking with till the end:

Ultimately, we either live with a moral code or we don't. And if you don't, if you think you can get away with treating people or animals or any living thing like they don't matter, you're delusional.

On my ranch outside Austin, I spend a lot of time with my rescue horses. They've got something to say to me just like I've got something to say to them. We speak in a language without words. It isn't that I don't love words—I do—but words can only go so far. Those horses take me to another place.

Ultimately, we either live with a moral code or we don't.

LOVE HAS A MIND OF ITS OWN

I forget exactly what "determinism" means, but it sounds like a word I should be using right about now. I'm pulling out the dictionary and looking it up . . .

"A doctrine that claims all human actions are determined by causes external to the will."

Hmmm . . .

But don't we have free will?

Or is it the way Fred Foster and Kris Kristofferson put it in their "Me and Bobby McGee": "Freedom is just another word for nothing left to lose."

If we lose love, have we lost everything? Hard to say because love contains so many opposites: It can be sacred and salty, lofty and lusty, self-centered and self-sacrificing, smart and stupid, helpful and hurtful, hopeful and hopeless, calm and chaotic. The yins and yangs of love are like the waves of the ocean. They never stop washing ashore.

Love moves at its own pace and goes wherever it wants to go. So maybe I agree with this business of determinism. Love is determined to do whatever the hell it wants to do. Don't get in its way. If you do, you'll be fighting fate, which is a little like fighting Muhammad Ali in his prime.

LOVE HAS A MIND OF ITS OWN

Forgetting you, darling, is not my
decision
For love has a mind of its own

I'd love to forget every time that you
kissed me
I'd love to forget that you're gone
And I'd gladly hold back each tear that
I'm crying
But love has a mind of its own

Love is the ruler, the greatest of kings
Love sits up high on a throne
Forgetting you, darling, is not my
decision
For love has a mind of its own

I don't want to carry this worrisome
heartache
I don't want to cry all night long
I wish I could run from the day that I
met you
But love has a mind of its own

This was written in what Hank Cochran, my partner in musical crime, used to call "The Weeping Willie Days."

"If I didn't know you as such a happy-go-lucky guy," said Hank, "I'd worry about you taking a long walk off a short pier."

Like a lot of people, I've struggled with dark days. In the early sixties, only a few years before I recorded this song, I thought it was a good idea to lie down in the middle of a downtown Nashville street. It was midnight, and I was drunk out of my mind. Freezing wind, snow coming down, and me in nothing but jeans and a denim jacket. Because there was hardly any traffic, I couldn't call it a full-out suicide attempt. But whatever it was, I sure as hell was tempting fate.

Maybe like the character I invented in "Love Has a Mind of Its Own," I realized I was no longer in control of my thinking. I was trying to forget what couldn't be forgotten: the fact that, back then, I'd written scores of songs that hadn't sold. By the time I was making a little money, I saw that much of my currency was in sadness. The sad songs sold.

To generate that currency wasn't hard. Hank wasn't wrong to see me as happy-go-lucky. I've always tried to be cheerful. But I'm also a storehouse of sadness with an inventory of melancholy merchandise that never gets depleted.

Why? I don't know. And I'm not sure I want to know.

I realized I was no longer in control of my thinking.

VALENTINE

Valentine
Won't you be my valentine
And introduce your heart to mine
And be my valentine

Summertime, we could run and play
Like summertime
With storybooks and nursery rhymes
So be my valentine

Candy heart, if anyone could, you could have a candy heart
You're the sweetest of all sweethearts
Won't you give your heart to me
Can't you see

I love you valentine
Won't you be my valentine
And won't you share your space with mine
And be my valentine

Don Was, always comfortable in the studio.

In 1993, Bill Clinton, who could play the blues on tenor sax, was in the White House. The Dallas Cowboys beat the Buffalo Bills and won the Super Bowl for the first time in fifteen years. I was in the studio with music maven Don Was doing *Across the Borderline*. Don's a great bass player and producer. He lets the artist be the artist. He also does all he can to bring out the best in the artist. He brought me songs by Kris Kristofferson, Bob Dylan, Paul Simon, Willie Dixon, Ry Cooder, Lyle Lovett, Peter Gabriel, Mose Allison, and John Hiatt. I loved them all and sang them without reservation. These were among the best writers in the business. But Don felt I needed to add a composition of my own.

I didn't have anything handy, but it so happened that Valentine's Day was right around the corner. It occurred to me that I'd never written a song celebrating that sweet holiday. I remembered grade school when we exchanged handwritten cards. I was hoping that little girl on whom I had a crush might favor me with one.

I tried writing with the heart of that hopeful five-year-old boy back there in Abbott, Texas.

When I wrote it and sang it on *Across the Borderline*, my oldest son Lukas was just about that age. If Lukas liked it, I figured I was okay. He did. When I heard him tell his mom, "Ask Daddy to sing that candy heart song," I'd say, "That's your mom's song, son. She's my valentine."

A MOMENT ISN'T VERY LONG

Yesterday as I talked with a friend in town
I forgot to remember that you'd gone
And for a moment I found myself smiling
But a moment isn't very long

And last night as I danced with a stranger
And she held her cheek close to my own
For a moment I almost forgot you
But a moment isn't very long

Every now and then I get a chance to smile
But those "every now and thens" only last a little while
And tonight I've got a date with a new love
But I know I'd do just as well at home

For a moment maybe I could forget you
But a moment isn't very long

If I'm wearing you out with too much philosophical nonsense, go on and skip this page and move on to the next song.

But I remember writing this thing and thinking, "Man, this is deep." I usually don't have that thought. I usually just move from writing the lyrics to finding the melody. These lyrics, though, gave me pause.

I'm guessing this story came to me when I was thirty-two or thirty-three, churning out material that producers were struggling to fit into the Nashville mold.

I'd read enough Eastern thought to know that one of the cornerstones of wisdom was to be in the now. Be in the moment. Don't look back and don't look ahead. Anchor yourself in present time because time is always present. The moment is eternal.

But is it?

Maybe that works if you're a guru sitting in your ashram, but how about the guy in Waco who's just lost his gal? He can try to center himself in present time. He can forget her for a moment. But, as the song says, a moment flies by. Try as he might, his mind moves back to other moments. Those moments stretch into hours, days, even weeks.

Finding that moment of peace where you forgive and forget is a good goal. If you can achieve it, that's beautiful. If you can't, welcome to the human race.

I LET MY MIND WANDER

I let my mind wander
And what did it do?
It just kept right on going
Until it got back to you

I can't trust it one minute
It's worse than a child
Disobeys without conscience
And it's driving me wild

When I let my mind wander
I try to keep my mind busy
With thoughts of today
But invariably memories seem to lure it away

My lonely heart wonders
If there'll ever come a day
A day I can be happy
But I don't see a way

Because I let my mind wander
I try to keep my mind busy
With thoughts of today
But invariably memories seem to lure it away

I have a warm feeling for this song because it wandered over to Ray Price, who first recorded it in 1967. Nothing could have made me happier. Ray was the best.

Earlier I mentioned that Ray had invited me into his legendary band, the Cherokee Cowboys. I didn't hesitate for a second.

"Only thing is," said Ray, "you'll have to play bass. You know how, don't you, Willie?"

"Sure thing," I lied.

On the way to the first gig, pedal steel guitarist and musical genius Jimmy Day taught me enough bass to keep me from getting laughed off the stage. Ray was big on presentation. He had us wearing matching glitter-and-sparkle Western costumes made by Nudie's of Hollywood. Man, I was living the life.

Written before I joined the Cherokee Cowboys, "I Let My Mind Wander" is another song in the mold of my-mind-goes-in-one-direction-and-heart-goes-in-another. When Ray recorded it, he set a slow, melancholy tempo. With that mournful, mellow sound of his, he had me crying tears of joy.

Subsequently, I cut it a couple of times on my own. And though it was my song, I couldn't help but hear it as Ray's. He embodied it. He turned it into a living thing. Ray died in 2013, and three years later I put out the album *For the Good Times*, my tribute to my mentor. Kristofferson, who wrote the title tune, had an attitude that mirrored mine. "Ray's version was good enough to establish me as a reputable songwriter," said Kris. "I must have sung it ten thousand times myself, but never without thinking of the man who made it a hit."

IT ALWAYS WILL BE

Sometimes I think
That love is somewhere
Living on an island all alone

I can see it in the darkness
I can feel it in the distance
And then it's gone

And then I know that it is time
For me to go and find my favorite girl
'Cause when I look into her eyes I see
All the love there is in all the world

And it always will be

There are some things I think about
And every time I do it breaks my heart
And there is nothing I can do
About this loneliness I feel when we're apart

I stop and curse the darkness and the distance
And then your face I see
And when I look into your eyes I see
All the love there is inside of me

And it always will be

I need to talk more about Ray Price.

On his last album, *Beauty Is . . . The Final Sessions*, he sang "It Always Will Be." When I heard it, I couldn't hold back the tears. Merle Haggard had sung it before and sang it beautifully. But Ray, realizing that the sun was about to set, treated the song as a prayer. He found the balance between grief and grace. He sang with the aching tenderness of a man—who could have been me, or Merle, or Ray himself—who knew the pain of being both connected and disconnected from a love we've all been seeking since that first day we wrote our first song.

Ray Price knew about life. He knew about longing. Like a great actor, he knew never to overplay his part. He sang with quiet intention. He sang with heartbreaking sincerity. He sang the truth.

On my tribute album to Ray, I recorded "It Always Will Be." I made it a point to use the same studio—Ocean Way in Nashville—where, three years earlier, Ray cut his perfect interpretation.

Why redo it if I thought Ray's version was perfect? It was my way of bringing Ray back. I needed to be close to him and feel the presence of his sweet spirit.

Now I hear "It Always Will Be" as a coda to our friendship. I'll never forget the man who put me on the map by taking an obscure song called "Night Life" and turning it into a hit. Today, Ray Price's musical heart beats as strongly as ever. He is forever.

With my mentor, Ray Price.

OPPORTUNITY TO CRY

Just watch the sunrise on the other side of town
Once more I've waited and once more you've let me down
This would be a perfect time for me to die
So I'd like to take this opportunity to cry

You gave your word now I return it to you
With this suggestion as to what you can do
Just exchange the words I love you to goodbye
While I take this opportunity to cry

I'd like to see you but I'm afraid
That I don't know wrong from right
And if I saw you would I kiss you
Or want to kill you on sight?

It's been a long night so I think I'll go home
And feed my nightmares
They've been waiting all night long
They'll be the last ones to tell me goodbye
And they'll give me many opportunities to cry

You won't be surprised that Hank Cochran put this song at the top of his "Weeping Willie Days" list.

"Damn, Willie," he said, "you're singing about maybe committing suicide and maybe killing off your girlfriend while you're crying your eyes out. You're sure you're okay?"

"I will be if it's a hit."

It wasn't. I recorded it for Liberty Records in 1963. Some twenty years later I recorded it again on *Pancho & Lefty*, an album I made with Merle Haggard. The original intention was to sing it as a duet, but Merle said, "I'd better leave this one alone. You sing it. If I do it, I might wind up doing what the song says to do."

"It's just a song, Merle."

"Your songs are more than songs, Willie. They're little plays where sometimes the endings are so unhappy, I get all messed up."

The Holmes Brothers, a great gospel/blues group, were happy to sing it with me on the TV special *Outlaws and Angels*. They gave it extra grit and porfoct harmony. Tom Jones recorded his own soulful version. And naturally I had to include it on *The IRS Tapes: Who'll Buy My Memories*, the album I made to help pay off my taxes. When you're looking at a mind-boggling tax bill, there's no better opportunity to cry.

"They're little plays where sometimes the endings are so unhappy, I get all messed up."

SHE'S NOT FOR YOU

Pay no mind to her
She only wants to play
She's not for you
She's not for you

And I'm the only one
Who would let her act this way
She's not for you
She's not for you

So she told you she found
Heaven in your eyes
Well I think it only fair
To warn you
Sometimes she lies

But it's your heart
I can't tell you what to do
She's not for you

She just looks for
Greener pastures now and then
And when she grows tired
She knows Old Faithful
Will just take her back again

So just leave her here
I'm used to feeling blue
She's not for you
She's not for you

They called Porter Wagoner "Mr. Grand Ole Opry." His national TV show, starting in 1960, ran for over twenty years. As everyone knows, it's where Dolly Parton became a star.

The same cannot be said of me. I appeared on Porter's show in the early black-and-white days. This was the clean-shaven Willie with a narrow lapel suit and skinny black tie. I'd just been to the barber, so my wavy hair was in place. I looked okay, but nothing could compete with Porter's famous pompadour.

I appreciated being invited on the show and sang "She's Not for You" in my usual simple manner. I received polite compliments, yet my career stayed stalled.

I never gave up on the song. Fact is, I never gave up on any of my songs. I sang "She's Not for You" on *Shotgun Willie* in 1973 and on *Across the Borderline* in 1993. I hope this doesn't sound like bragging, but I don't see my songs as aging, especially this one.

Men will always be desperate to keep a woman they are afraid of losing. They will always warn other men to stay away. They will list the lady's faults. And they will always know in their hearts that, despite those faults, they will take her back.

Love dies hard. Or maybe it doesn't die at all. Or maybe men, at least some men, are fatally attracted to women who will never do right by them. And those men, knowing their fate, continue to love even harder.

I THOUGHT I LEFT YOU

I thought I left you
What part of "we can't make it" don't you
    understand?
It's no longer you and me, there's another
    world we'll see
I thought I left you, so why aren't you leaving
    me?

I thought I left you
What part of "it's all over" don't you
    understand?
You fell out of love with me so I moved on
    quietly
I thought I left you, so why aren't you leaving
    me?

You're like the measles,
You're like the whooping cough
I've already had you
So why in heaven's name can't you just
    get lost?

I thought I left you
So don't you think it's time you're leaving me?
I thought I left you
So don't you think it's time you let me leave?

The bus is leaving, it's already left the parking
    lot
And I checked the list to see if you were on it
Searched around and thankfully you're not

I thought I left you
Don't you think it's time you're leaving me?
I thought I left you
Don't you think it's time you let me be?

Here's proof that the more things change, the more they stay the same.

I sang this song at a concert not long ago. After the show, an especially kind fan came up to me and said, "Willie, I've loved that song ever since you started singing it back in the old days. It's my favorite of all your old songs."

I thanked him and didn't bother to correct him. No reason to make a fan feel bad. The truth is, though, I didn't write the song with Buddy Cannon until 2013 for my *Band of Brothers* album. I also didn't correct the fan because it does, in fact, sound like an old song. Maybe all my songs sound old. And that doesn't bother me a bit. I say that because most of my songs are about old feelings.

When I sing "I Thought I Left You," I get a feeling of confusion. Who's leaving who? So many love affairs get lost in confusion.

Can she ever let you go? Can you ever let her go?

Love has a way of lingering. And it's my hope that songs like this, though they might sound like they were written a lifetime ago, have that same lingering effect.

The emotions that draw lovers together can be like a monsoon. The rain keeps falling, day after day, month after month, until you start thinking you'll never see the sun again. You're lost in a steady downpour of doubt. And if your lover does leave you, or if you leave her, you won't know whether you're sad or glad. All you'll know is that the rain keeps coming down.

Maybe all my songs sound old.

HEALING HANDS OF TIME

They're working while I'm missing you
Those healing hands of time
And soon they'll be dismissing you
From this heart of mine

They'll lead me safely through the night
And I'll follow as though blind
My future tightly clutched within
Those healing hands of time

They let me close my eyes just then
Those healing hands of time
And soon they'll let me sleep again
Those healing hands of time

So already I've reached mountain peaks
And I've just begun to climb
I'll get over you by clinging to
Those healing hands of time

This is a song I'm never going to stop singing because I'm never going to stop needing the lesson it's teaching.

It isn't a lesson that I concocted. It's a lesson I've learned through living. I wrote it early in my life and was blessed that it was recorded in 1966 by Ray Price. Ray keeps coming back into the picture. His presence comforts me.

Ray was seven years my senior. He had wisdom I lacked, not only as a man but as a singer. Just as he had deepened "Night Life," "I Let My Mind Wander," and "It Will Always Be," he took "Healing Hands of Time" to another place. He took the song beyond time. He understood that time is flowing energy and if you go with the flow your worst wounds will mend. That certain knowledge is all in Ray's voice. As much as in the lyrics, there is healing in the sound of Ray's voice.

I recorded it in 1976 on *The Sound in Your Mind* and again in 1994 on the album actually called *Healing Hands of Time*. That was the one and only time I wore a tux for a cover photo. Producer Jimmy Bowen surrounded the song with such lush, sophisticated strings that I wanted to show some respect and, for once, get dressed up.

My favorite version, other than Ray's, may be one where I sure as hell did *not* get dressed up. I recorded it in a home studio with my boys Lukas and Micah. We each sang a verse and harmonized on the chorus. It was during the pandemic, when we needed to remember that, even in the face of catastrophe, time does, in fact, heal.

With Ray and legendary bassist Michael Rhodes.

ABANDONED HOUSES

Elvis didn't write "Heartbreak Hotel." Mae Boren Axton did. I met her when I was deejaying up in Oregon on KVAN. I was twenty-four years old and fashioned myself a writer. Ms. Axton worked as a promotion lady for Colonel Parker, who was managing both Elvis and Hank Snow. In the early days, Elvis was opening for Hank.

When she showed up at the station, I wanted to play her some of my own songs, but before I did, I asked her about how she came up with "Heartbreak Hotel."

"Run-down hotels, seedy motels, and abandoned houses—they all make for good songs," she said.

That gave me pause to play her the one song I'd written that had nothing to do with run-down hotels, seedy motels, or abandoned houses. It was more or less a religious song: "Family Bible."

I got past my hesitation and played it for her anyway. She liked it and advised me to get out of Oregon and head to Nashville. It took me a while to build up the nerve, but I did make that move.

In the meantime, I never forgot what she told me and wound up using homes and houses, hotels and motels, and even lonely little mansions in so many of my songs that they merit a category all their own.

WHERE MY HOUSE LIVES

Stop here . . .
Across the street to your right
That's where my house lives
Sometimes I stayed there at night

But mostly I was on the move
Business first you know
And she'd wait there in her lonely room
But oh that's been so long ago

She's gone now . . .
She couldn't stand to be alone
And now it waits there
This house that used to be my home

I never go there 'cause it holds
Too many memories since she's gone
But right there is where
My house lives all alone

Every story has a home.

One night, with nothing better to do, I started to list all the places where I'd ever lived. I started in Abbott, moved on to Tyler and Waco, and by the time I got to Fort Worth I got tired and gave up.

A lot of those places, especially Abbott, held many beautiful memories, but many of them didn't. When I wrote "Where My House Lives" in the early sixties, I'd been reminiscing about the many places I had inhabited and abandoned. Houses are our shelter against the storms of life. Houses are where children grow up and spouses share precious times. Houses stand as monuments to faithfulness. When the faithfulness dies, the house is never the same.

Women are more patient than men. Women are wiser than men. Women will keep the faith when men have long abandoned it. Women keep the home fires burning. Men, on the other hand, are inclined to an attitude of out of sight, out of mind. They remember the house fondly, but they're too caught up in themselves, too busy chasing after things that are forever elusive, to realize what they've lost.

You lose a woman.

You lose a house.

You lose your soul.

And if, in the process, you're able to write about it, that doesn't mean the loss doesn't sting. The song makes the loss sting a little less.

Houses stand as monuments to faithfulness.

HAPPINESS LIVES NEXT DOOR

I'm sorry, but you've come to the wrong house
But I know who those flowers are for
The flowers that you have are for someone who's happy
And happiness lives next door

Someone sends her flowers each evening
And her young heart is flooded with joy
So don't keep her waiting, deliver the flowers
To happiness who lives next door

The only one who would send flowers to me
Is gone to return no more
But there's some consolation to know someone is happy
And happiness lives next door

I like Judy Garland. Who doesn't? Judy had soul. Hearing her sing "Over the Rainbow" in *The Wizard of Oz* was something I never forgot. I also remember her singing "The Boy Next Door" in *Meet Me in St. Louis.* That's probably not where I got the idea for "Happiness Lives Next Door," but who knows where ideas come from?

It's a tantalizing notion: love being this close and, at the same time, that far. It's water water everywhere but not a drop to drink. It's sweet torture. I put myself in songs like this not because it actually happened to me but because it sure as hell could have. It's the way love works.

You're sitting alone in a movie theater. She comes and sits next to you. Your heart starts dancing. She gives you a glance. You're sure. You're convinced. Fate is finally delivering. And just as you're about to reach over and take her hand, he arrives. They embrace. You deflate.

The house of love crumbles. So, you head out to the lumberyard and build yourself a bigger house, a better house. You paint it white and put up a cute little picket fence. You leave the door wide open. Love will surely drop by. It's just a matter of waiting. But, meanwhile, in the midnight hour when sleep won't come, you put your hands over your ears. The sound of the couple making love next door is more than you can stand.

LONELY LITTLE MANSION

Furnished with everything but love
I'm looking for someone to come live
   in me
I've got a large picture window
And a yard filled with trees

The sign reads "two stories"
And that's all that's for sale
But there's so many stories I could tell

My windows are closed and I'm
   gasping for air
My carpets are spotted
With tearstains here and there

A torn photograph still lies on my floor
And two sweethearts
Don't live here anymore

I'm a lonely little mansion for sale
And for someone I'd fit just like a glove
I'm a lonely little mansion for sale
Furnished with everything but love

Here's something I don't do very much: I turn myself into a house and let the house sing the song.

Don't ask me why. At the time, it just felt like a good idea. Or maybe, having written about houses so much, I decided that this time the house had more to say than I did.

When I first wrote "Hello Walls," I got criticized for talking to inanimate objects like walls, windows, and ceilings. Some said it was dumb. Then when Faron Young turned it into a hit, everyone said it was smart.

Walls, windows, and ceilings are pieces of a house. A whole house is something different. I believe a house, like a person, has a soul. A house has a history. A house contains memories. A house is the stage for countless scenes between families coming together and falling apart.

Once I was in Galveston. It was early afternoon. I'd played a gig the night before and had just enjoyed a good breakfast, and I went for a walk. The weather was fine. I felt fine. All seemed right with the world . . . until I happened to pass by a street where a bulldozer was tearing down one of those big old houses from a previous era. A massive concrete ball was smashing out the windows. The porch crumbled. The roof collapsed. Dust flew everywhere.

And tears streamed down my face.

I believe a
house, like
a person,
has a soul.

MISERY MANSION

Misery mansion so cold and so gray
You look so lonely since she went away
Misery mansion what secrets you hide
Of a love that has faded and died

Misery mansion, oh how you've changed
Your walls hold the sorrow that loneliness
   brings
A love of a lifetime forever is gone
Misery mansion my home

You know all the reasons why she said
   goodbye
And you stand there in silence while I sit
   and cry
Misery mansion we're both so alone
Misery mansion my home

In this song, one of the first I ever wrote, I change direction.

I don't let the house talk to me.

I talk to the house. And, though it might be unfair, I don't let the house talk back.

I want the house to feel my pain. I want the house to comfort me and be my friend. I'm sick and tired of being sick and tired. I want to be housed in love. But this house is cold. It won't say a word.

I have a good friend in Austin who's been a real estate agent for fifty years. He was in the right place at the right time. As Austin grew from a sleepy college town to a thriving metropolis, he made a small fortune. He once told me that the secret in selling a house was his opening line.

"Soon as I escort the prospective buyers inside," he said, "my first words to the couple are, 'You're going to love this place. This is going to be more than a house. This is going to be a home. This is where you're going to be happy for the rest of your lives.'"

"And how many of those couples that bought those houses are still together?" I asked.

"My guess would be not very many."

I nodded my head, and that night wrote a song about another unhappy home.

I want the house to feel my pain.

I JUST DROPPED BY

I just dropped by to see the house I used to live in
I hope that you don't mind, I won't stay very long
So long ago someone and I lived here together
And then so suddenly I found myself alone

I couldn't stand the thought of living here without her
And so I moved away to let my memories die
But my memories outlived my better judgment
This may sound strange to you but I just thought I'd drop by

The very door you're standing in, she used to stand there
And wait for me to come home every night
And when I'd see her standing there I'd run to meet her
These things were on my mind so I just thought I'd drop by

I guess that I should leave, someone just might not understand
And I'm aware of how the neighbors like to pry
But you can tell them all today a most unhappy man
Was in the neighborhood and he just thought he'd drop by

I'm changing directions again, and I'm wondering if you've done the same thing. Have you driven around your old neighborhood?

You have no intention to stop by the house where you used to live, but something makes you change direction. You turn around and park in front. You're not going inside. You're just going to sit there and look. Going inside would be too painful.

The curtains are open, though, and you can see people in the living room. You hear a dog bark. You hear children laughing. You find yourself getting out of your car and walking to the front door. You stand there for a full minute before you ring the bell.

A woman opens the door. A man stands next to her. He's half your age. She's even younger. The kids come around. Their parents politely ask what you want. All you can say is, "I used to live here."

These strangers couldn't be sweeter. They invite you in. "Look around. Take all the time you need." They love the house. They're sure that you once loved it as well.

You see the kitchen, the tiny den. You walk into the backyard. The dog licks your hand. Inside, the kids' bedrooms are crowded with stuffed animals and building blocks. What about the master bedroom? What about that sacred place where you and she loved so passionately that you knew your love would last forever? Can you go back there? Can you even look inside that room?

No. You avoid it. You thank the kind folks and go on your way.

SPIRIT

"Off-the-cuff" might not sound like a spiritual concept, but it's one of the working principles that has allowed spirit to guide me.

For reasons I can't explain, some of the best things happen to me off-the-cuff. Things that feel right. And when they do, I just leave them alone. I let them be.

The album I called *Spirit* is a good example. It was 1996. I was about to turn sixty-three. We were off the road. I was just getting over a bad bout with the flu. My voice was strained. So, I decided to take a few weeks and stay on my Texas ranch. Play a little golf. Play a little poker. Relax.

One day I wandered over to the studio and started fooling around. By chance, sister Bobbie, Jody Payne, and Johnny Gimble wandered in.

"What are you up to, Willie?" asked Bobbie.

"Just feel like playing. Y'all play along if you want to."

Bobbie went to the piano, Jody picked up his guitar, and Johnny took out his fiddle. Naturally, I had Trigger in my arms and a couple of songs in my head. Some were new, some were old. Figured it wouldn't hurt to record what we were doing, just in case.

After cutting three or four songs, we played them back. They sounded like demos rather than completed productions. I liked that sound. I didn't mind that my voice, still recovering from the flu, was more restrained than usual. I liked the feeling of that restraint. I decided not to add strings or horns. I didn't call an arranger and didn't feel like I needed a producer.

A spirit was emerging. To honor that spirit required doing as little as possible.

After a few days, we had a dozen or so songs.

I presented the music to the label. They weren't sure. I was.

This was spirit, pure and simple.

SHE IS GONE

She is gone
But she was here
And her presence is still heavy
   in the air

Oh what a taste
Of human love
Now she's gone and it don't
   matter anymore

Passing dreams
In the night
It was more than just a woman
   and a man

It was love
Without disguise
And now my life will never be
   the same again

A man with a snow-white beard is wearing a slightly frayed cowboy hat. He holds a beat-up Martin N-20 guitar covered with scores of signatures. In a barren field, he stands on a sloping section of brown grass. Behind him is a low stone wall. Beyond the walls are leafless trees. It's early winter. The film capturing his performance is grainy. As he starts to sing, he looks directly into the camera. Looking down at his guitar, he appears peaceful and, at the same time, projects an air of sadness. Or maybe it's resignation. You'd recognize the man as me. In this video, I'm singing "She Is Gone."

Like so many of my songs, the main character—"She"—remains unidentified.

Her identity becomes clear when, after the song is released, I get lots of letters and emails.

"When I heard you sing it, Willie, my mind went back to the daughter I lost . . ."

"I took the song to be about my wife who died last year . . ."

"Mama's death was rough, but this song really helped me get through it . . ."

"I know you were singing about my sister . . ."

Seems like everyone took it personally.

And nothing could please me more.

The late forties. That's me, second from the left, holding a guitar, and sister Bobbie, looking pretty as a picture.

YOUR MEMORY WON'T DIE IN MY GRAVE

Been feeling kind of free
But I sure do feel lonesome
Baby's taking a trip
But she ain't takin' me

I've been feeling kinda free
But I'd rather feel your arms around me
'Cause you're taking away
Everything that I wanted

There's an old hollow tree
Where we carved our initials
And I said I love you
And you said you love me

It's a memory today
It'll be a memory tomorrow
I hope you'll be happy someday
Your memory won't die in my grave

Spirit has nothing to do with logic. I can lose a love and feel free about it.

Love carries burdens. Love causes crazy thinking. To escape crazy thinking can be liberating.

Love's gone, but so are the sorrows that accompanied it.

But the sorrows stick around and the freedom no longer feels like freedom at all. The loss leads to a loneliness that seems like it'll last forever.

Spirit has nothing to do with common sense.

Common sense says cut your losses and move on. Common sense says what happened yesterday doesn't have to mess up today. Today is new and fresh and alive with promises.

Spirit has everything to do with truth. True spirit lives inside you. You can try and run from it. You can feel sorry for yourself. You can practically drown in your own tears. Or you can convince yourself that sadness is something you can control. You can cut off the sadness whenever you want.

Except you can't. Memories are made of spirit. They're like the stars in the sky. Every time you look up, they'll be there. They twinkle and shine and glow with a light that can't be extinguished.

Spirit contains all the mysteries, all the memories, all the passion and sadness and joy and grief that defy time.

Spirit defies death.

On Mama and Daddy Nelson's porch: Bobbie and her then-husband Bud
Fletcher (standing), cousin Ronnie, me (holding dog), and cousin Ernestine.

I'M NOT TRYING TO FORGET YOU ANYMORE

I'm not trying to forget you anymore
I've got back into remembering all the love we had before
And I'd been trying to forget someone that my heart still adores
So I'm not trying to forget you anymore

You're just someone who brought happiness into my life
And it did not last forever, oh but that's all right
We were always more than lovers and I'm still your friend
And if I had the chance, I'd do it all again

So I'm not trying to forget you anymore
I've got back into remembering all the love we had before
And the best day of my life is still
When you walked through my door

So I'm not trying to forget you anymore

Sometime in the nineties, I'd just gotten off stage in Meridian, Mississippi, when a tall, thin guy wearing a sharp Western-style suit approached me and said, "I hate to bother you, Willie, but your music means the world to me and I'm wondering if I might have a minute of your time."

I invited him on the bus. When he told me he was a professional gambler, I wasn't surprised. He had that look. He didn't mince words. He confessed doing sleight of hand everywhere from Singapore to San Francisco. He'd never been caught. He said he'd done it all to escape the pain of losing the only woman he had ever loved, his high school sweetheart who'd tossed him aside and instead married his brother, a straight-A student and now a prosperous doctor in Atlanta. The gambler had been around the world, but never once been to visit his brother and sister-in-law and their three children.

"I've spent my life trying to forget her," he told me, "but I can't."

He sensed the question I was about to ask him—"Why are you telling me this?"—and answered it before I could get the words out of my mouth.

"Your music won't let me forget her," he said, brushing away a small tear from the corner of his eye. "And that's something I have to thank you for."

I nodded my head in appreciation. After we shook hands, he walked off the bus and I never saw him again.

TOO SICK TO PRAY

I've been too sick to pray, Lord
That's why we ain't talked in a while
It's been some of them days, Lord
I thought I was on my last mile

But I'm feeling okay, Lord
And I'm glad that I called you today
Never needed you more
I would have called you before
But I've been too sick to pray

Remember the family, Lord?
I know they will remember you
And all of their prayers, Lord
They talk to you just like I do

Well, I reckon that's all, Lord
That's all I can think of to say
And thank you, my friend,
We'll be talking again
If I'm not too sick to pray

I'd never tell anyone how to pray, since I'm not sure how to pray myself.

Some people believe in prayers of solicitation.

Some such prayers might sound a little self-serving—"Dear Lord, let me land that deal"—while others might sound reasonable—"Dear Lord, restore my health."

I once heard a preacher say that the only solicitation prayers he liked were those asking God for more love and compassion.

I can understand how anyone in a state of desperation wants to reach out to a holy power for relief. I've never adopted any one formula for prayer.

Yet after writing this song I called "Too Sick to Pray," I had a realization: In some way, all my songs are prayers. All my songs are ways to tap into something greater than myself. That something is music. Music gives me relief. And if you were to call music God, I wouldn't argue. In times of both trouble and celebration, I've always turned to music. It's my channel to the Great Unknown.

"I'm too sick to pray" is a strange statement. That statement *is* a prayer. So is the song. I'm too sick to be doing the very thing I'm doing, yet in doing it I'm addressing God in the best way I know how.

I'm singing.

And if you
were to call
music God,
I wouldn't
argue.

I'M WAITING FOREVER

I'm waiting forever for you
For this is my destiny
This is what I am to do

But forever ain't no time at all
It's only the time
Between telephone calls

And the love that I hear
In your voice is so clear
Coming through
Keeps me waiting forever
Waiting forever for you

I'm waiting forever for you
For this is my destiny
This is what I am to do

Waiting is no waste of time
I just play out the scenes
On a stage in my mind

And I love making love to your memory
It's all that I do
While I'm waiting forever
Waiting forever for you

As a former Bible school teacher, I give myself the right to quote Scripture a couple times in this book:

"Conduct yourselves with all humility, gentleness, and patience." —Ephesians 4:2.

Of those three qualities, patience might be the most important. When impatience is bubbling inside you, it's hard to be either humble or gentle. But the thing about patience is this: Just when you're sure you've been patient enough, you've got to be even more patient. Like love, pure patience is infinite.

We're impatient to connect. We're impatient with this whole uncertain unprovable spiritual process.

So I seek solace in waiting. I say waiting is the permanent condition. Waiting is a sacred act. Waiting—without bemoaning or bitching—is a testimony to faith.

When do we ever stop waiting?

We wait for a deliverance that, even if it arrives, we aren't sure is real.

We wait for a sign from above that, when it appears, can be interpreted a million different ways.

Embracing the wait might be the only way of realizing the beauty of the wait.

The wait might be the distance between heaven and earth.

It's incalculable.

Waiting—without bemoaning or bitching—is a testament to faith.

WE DON'T RUN

We don't run, we don't compromise
We don't quit, we never do
We look for love, we find it in the eyes
The eyes of me and the eyes of you

You are the road, you are the only way
I'll follow you forever more
We'll look for love, we'll find it in the eyes
The eyes that see through all the doors

There is a train that races through the night
On rails of steel that reach the soul
Fueled by fire as soft as candlelight
But it warms the heart of a love grown cold

And we don't run and we don't compromise
We don't quit, we never do
We look for love, we find it in the eyes
The eyes of me and the eyes of you

Words that feel, words that sympathize
Words that heal and understand
Say them now, let them materialize
Say the words throughout the land

The old expression says, "You can run, but you can't hide."

"But you're a runner, Willie," a friend reminded me.

"Used to be. When my knees were still strong, I ran all the time."

"So how did you come to write a song that says, 'We don't run'? Hell, you've been running up and down the road your whole life."

"It's from this album I called *Spirit*," I said. "It's a record where I just tried to let spirit take over."

"Sounds like the spirit came on strong in this song. It's got you staying in place to fight the good fight."

"Is that how you see it?" I asked.

"I guess. But how do you see it?"

"Some famous writer—can't remember who—said, 'Don't trust the teller. Trust the tale.'"

"But a lot of your tales are downright convoluted. In this one you got these rails of steel running through your soul. What's all that about, Willie?"

"You tell me."

"I don't know. Might not be anything more than the fact that you're stubborn about standing your ground. Does that explain it?"

"Maybe yes, maybe no."

I GUESS I'VE COME TO LIVE HERE IN YOUR EYES

I guess I've come to live here in your eyes
This must be the place called paradise
You are so precious to me, what a special
    time within our lives
I guess I've come to live here in your eyes

A thousand times I see you
And a thousand times you take my
    breath away
Fears and doubts consume me
And I'm afraid someone will take it all
    away

I hope I'm here forever
But I think it's time that we both realize
And I guess I've come to live here
    in your eyes

Sometimes I don't do what I set out to do.

In 1979, when we were planning the movie *Honeysuckle Rose*, we needed a lot of songs, and I wanted to write some new ones. Many would be filmed before audiences. It wasn't a musical, so the songs didn't have to advance any plotline.

I figured I'd write a simple love song. Though I wasn't exactly sure what it meant, I liked the way the title sounded: "I Guess I've Come to Live Here in Your Eyes." That sounded like a nice place to live.

Any writer will tell you that's a safe bet to praise your lover in a song. "You're beautiful, you're special, you're my dream come true, I've never known a love like this." Such sentiments were my intention, but, me being me, I got derailed.

I suddenly felt that this guy, wanting to sweet-talk his lady with words of appreciation, had big-time apprehensions. I heard him say that he was consumed by fear. Maybe that's why he "guesses"—but doesn't know—that he'll come to live in the eyes of his lady. Maybe he will and maybe he won't.

Maybe having to live in someone's eyes is different than living with someone, body and soul. Maybe when the singer sees a reflection of himself in that someone's eyes, he sees a man who, though deeply in love, is just as deeply in doubt.

When I put together the album *Spirit*, I included this song. I thought it fit with the theme of knowing that you don't know.

HONEYSUCKLE ROSE

For 20 years he's been singing
to the country.

But he never figured
he'd be living his own love songs.

A SYDNEY POLLACK/GENE TAFT Production A JERRY SCHATZBERG Film
WILLIE NELSON
DYAN CANNON AMY IRVING
HONEYSUCKLE ROSE
Also starring SLIM PICKENS Executive Producer SYDNEY POLLACK
Screenplay by CAROL SOBIESKI and WILLIAM D. WITTLIFF and JOHN BINDER
Based on the story by GOSTA STEVEN and GUSTAV MOLANDER Produced by GENE TAFT
Original songs composed by WILLIE NELSON and performed by WILLIE NELSON and FAMILY
Directed by JERRY SCHATZBERG

IT'S A DREAM COME TRUE

It's a dream come true
I can't believe that it's just me
    and you
Seeing worlds so far apart
Come together in our hearts
It's a dream come true

It's a dream come true
There is nothing that a dream
    can't do
I dreamed of love and I was
    given you
You're a dream come true

These are changing times
A universe within our minds
With all the power of a love divine
It's a dream come true

It's a symphony
And all the notes ring out in
    harmony
It's the music of the stars
It fulfills all my desires

It's a dream come true
It's the music of the stars
It fulfills all my desires
It's a dream come true

I mentioned Zeke Varnon, the man who, when I was sixteen, introduced me to the pleasures and pitfalls of living the daredevil life. He used to come by the Nite Owl, a club where sister Bobbie and I were playing in a band led by Bud Fletcher, Bobbie's husband. That's where late one night Zeke told me a story about an army buddy. They were fighting overseas when his pal kept talking about his recurring dream of falling in love with a dark-eyed, dark-haired woman as beautiful as the Queen of Sheba.

When the American Fifth Army helped liberate Rome in the summer of 1944, Zeke's friend fell sick with severe pneumonia. He wound up in a hospital, where he almost died. At the last minute, he rallied. Still feverish, he woke up. He had no idea where he was. All he knew was that he was looking into the dark eyes of the woman he had dreamed about. His nurse looked like the Queen of Sheba. Then he closed his eyes and drifted back to sleep.

Days later, he gained full consciousness. The nurse had disappeared. All his attempts to find her failed. His buddies told him it was a just a dream, but he knew better.

He went home to Corpus Christi, where he worked in construction. Years passed. On a lunch break, he sat at the counter of a café, about to order a cheeseburger, when he looked up into the dark eyes of a waitress who looked like the Queen of Sheba. She spoke with a foreign accent. Having lost her family in the war, she had resettled in Texas. "Did you live in Rome? Did you work as a nurse?"

"Yes," was all she had to say.

I THOUGHT ABOUT YOU, LORD

I thought about trees
And how much I'd like to climb one
I thought about friends
And how rare it is to find one
I thought about you
The most gentle, sweet and kind one
I thought about you, Lord
I thought about you

I thought about life
And the way that things are going
I thought about love
And the pain there is in growing
And I thought about you
The one who is all-knowing
I thought about you, Lord
I thought about you

I thought about you
And the songs that I keep singing
I thought about you
And the joy that they keep bringing
I thought about life
And a love that has no ending
I thought about you, Lord
I thought about you

For a man who believes in the beauty of private prayer, I sure have done a lot of praying in public. I give myself the excuse that I put the prayers in songs because, like Mary Poppins says, a spoonful of sugar makes the medicine go down.

Sometimes I wonder why it's hard for some people to pray. I have friends who are atheists who think praying is no different than farting in the wind. I never argue with them. The minute you start an argument like that, you lose. Matter of fact, a good prayer would be never to argue about prayer. The same prayer would ask the Lord to keep you from arguing with anyone about the Lord.

When you play poker, there are winners and losers. That's fine. That's even fun, especially if you win. But when you're playing a mind game and the subject is something as serious as spirit, you don't want to win. If you do, if you've defeated your opponent and made him feel bad, you've lost.

Spirit needs to include, not exclude. Spirit needs to be positive, not negative. Spirit needs to bring folks up, not put them down.

The whole point—at least the way I see it—is to let spirit move through us. To do that, spirit needs to bypass the ego. The ego is great for certain things. We all need egos. But the ego usually needs to be right. The ego likes to assert itself and take command. Meanwhile, spirit is a quiet thing. Watch the bluebird fly through the sky. Listen to the babbling brook. When the sun sets, sometimes the sky turns pink, then purple, then deep blue. Night falls. The planet spins. There's so much out there. Spirit everywhere.

TEATRO

In 1988, if you drove about sixty miles northwest of LA on U.S. 1, you'd come to Oxnard, California. There you'd walk into a deserted old movie theater where they used to show Mexican films and you'd find me and a bunch of musicians working on an album cooked up by Daniel Lanois, a producer with a mind of his own. *Teatro* was Daniel's vision.

After self-producing *Spirit* a couple of years earlier, I was ready to hand over the reins, especially to someone like Daniel, who turned out to be deep into the songs I'd written in the sixties. He had his own peculiar way for me to reimagine them.

Imagine this: The seats have been pulled out of the theater. So have the rugs. The floor is concrete. The big screen is still there. The velvet curtains are worn and torn. A studio has been set up with a massive mixing board. Behind the board a row of baffles absorbs the sound. Lighting comes from flickering candles. Daniel makes all sorts of intriguing suggestions. Instead of playing acoustic, have Bobbie play electric piano. Have Mickey Raphael switch to echo harmonica to give the feel of an accordion. Bring in musicians like pianist Brad Mehldau, drummers Tony Mangurian and Victor Indrizzo, percussionist Cyril Neville, and guitarist Brian Griffiths. Get me to put Trigger aside and instead play a hollow-body electric. Let a flamenco feeling flow over everything. And then, to top it all, have the great Emmylou Harris harmonize my vocals.

We did the whole thing live. No overdubs. The playback mixes were the final mixes. Rough and raw and, to my ears, just the way to bring my old songs back to life. To shake things up a little more, I added a couple of new songs.

Daniel had no objections. He thought the concept held together.

"What is the concept?" I asked him.

"Strung together," he said, "these tunes tell a story."

"About what?"

"Searching. Longing. Loneliness."

I NEVER CARED FOR YOU

The sun is filled with ice and gives no warmth at all
And the sky was never blue
The stars are raindrops searching for a place to fall
And I never cared for you

I know you won't believe these things I tell you
I know you won't believe
Your heart has been forewarned all men will lie to you
And your mind cannot conceive

Now all depends on what I say to you
And on your doubting me
So I've prepared these statements far from true
Pay heed and disbelieve

The sun is filled with ice and gives no warmth at all
And the sky was never blue
The stars are raindrops searching for a place to fall
And I never cared for you

How do you deal with a song that tells you not to believe it?

How do you process feelings that you know are fake?

Seeing is supposed to be believing. The sun *is* warm. The sky *is* blue. Stars stay in the heavens and never land like raindrops.

When these words came to me, they didn't make sense. Like raindrops looking for a place to fall, they fell out of my head onto the page. And the one line that held them together was the biggest lie of all, a lie so outrageous it became the title.

Of course I cared for you. I loved you with all my heart. I would have given anything to have you believe me. But you were right to doubt me. You knew me. You knew men. You understand how we fabricate and deceive. You saw through my sarcasm, and as you listen to this song, you see how sarcasm hides all my true sentiments.

Does my sarcasm soften your resolve to stay away? Can you see that, by disbelieving me, you fooled yourself? I'm now asking you to pay heed and disregard my old deceptions. I want you back.

I'm coming clean but, in doing so, I can't help but protect myself. I'm saying what's not true—that I never cared for you—praying that this time you'll see through my lie.

EVERYWHERE I GO

I'll take you with me everywhere I go
I'll put you in my pocket, who will know?
Right next to my heart at every show
I'll take you with me everywhere I go

No matter where our trails will finally wind
Our paths will just keep crossing, yours and mine
Until then in my pocket you must go
I'll take you with me everywhere I go

The teatro is a sacred space.

In its emptiness, the actor—the singer, the musician—stands before an audience that is not present but is always present. The audience has been around for centuries. They've seen cowboy movies and Shakespearean tragedies. They've seen wrestling matches and grand opera, vaudeville acts and ballets and concerts by the world's greatest Spanish guitarists. They've seen and heard everything.

Once you connect with them, they become part of you. You become part of them.

You carry them into your solitude. You carry them into your dreams.

Riding a horse through a meadow overrun with wildflowers, I've gotten the feeling that everyone I'd ever sung to was there with me.

I've been alone at night, sitting on the porch and gazing at the sky while the sight of a shooting star thrilled my soul. In that moment, all the people in my life—some gone, some present, some still to come—were with me.

I can't explain it. I don't want to explain it. I just to need to say it:

You're with me everywhere I go.

Your energy. All energy.

It's beautiful.

With Emmylou Harris and Daniel Lanois.

DARKNESS ON THE FACE OF THE EARTH

The morning that you left me was just
    another day
How could I see the sorrow that had found
    me
Then you laughed and told me that I was
    in your way
And I turned and ran as heaven fell
    around me

I stumbled through the darkness, my
    footsteps were unsure
I lived within a world that had no sunshine
When you left me, darling, my world came
    to an end
And there was darkness on the face of the
    earth

The stars fell out of heaven and the moon
    could not be found
The sun was in a million pieces scattered
    all around
Why did you ever leave me, you knew
    how it would hurt
And now there's darkness on the face
    of the earth

In 1961, when I wrote this song, I was twenty-eight.

Chet Atkins, a great guitarist and legendary producer, had me under contract. He was trying to turn me into a star, but it wasn't working.

When I sang him this song, it was just me and my guitar.

"I like the lyrics," he said. "I like how the stars are falling out of heaven and the moon has disappeared. But the dang thing is so sad we're going to have to cheer it up."

I didn't object. Chet had produced dozens of hits, while I was batting zero. He added lots of sweetening, including lady background singers.

Thirty-seven years later, Daniel Lanois remembered the song and urged me to do it again. He gave it an upbeat Latin beat and, like Chet, found a way to counteract the melancholy mood of my message.

I again didn't object. With Emmylou shadowing me, the song took on an eerie character that had me thinking that there are lots of shades of darkness.

I was happy to rerecord it. Happy because I knew that, whatever had happened between ages twenty-eight and sixty-five, this dark little song had survived.

MY OWN PECULIAR WAY

It would be a comfort just to know you never doubt me
Even though I give you cause most every day
Sometimes I think that you'd be better off without me
Although I love you in my own peculiar way

Don't doubt my love if sometimes my mind should wander
To a suddenly remembered yesterday
But my mind could never stay too long away from you
And I'll always love you in my own peculiar way

Though I may not always be the way you'd have me be
Though my faults may grow in number day by day
Let no one ever say that I've ever been untrue
I'll always love you in my own peculiar way

I liked Perry Como. He had a silky-smooth, easygoing singing style that could relax a wild boar. He also had his own national TV show with big-name guests like Pearl Bailey and Lena Horne. So, when I learned he was going to cover "My Own Peculiar Way," I was flattered. He sang it softly. To my ears, he sang it beautifully.

That was 1965. I'd already recorded it on my first Liberty album in 1961 and then again in 1966 on a live album from Panther Hall in Fort Worth. In 1968, Chet Atkins, who also produced Perry Como's version, liked it well enough to use it as a title for my own album. That meant fooling with it again.

Like good people, good songs age well. Like good wines, good songs can mellow and go down even easier. In the late eighties when Daniel Lanois was putting together *Teatro*, he asked me whether I was tired of "My Own Peculiar Way."

"Might sound boastful," I said, "but I don't think I'm tired of singing any of my songs."

"It's got a funky feeling," said Daniel. "We might even be able to make it a tad funkier. Any objections?"

"Nope."

In that empty movie house, the song—and especially the line that said "my faults may grow in number day by day"—sounded new. I felt like I was singing it for the first time.

HOME MOTEL

What used to be my home has changed
To just a place to stay
A crumbling last resort when day is through

Sometimes between sundown and dawn
Somehow I find my way
To this Home Motel on Lost Love Avenue

No one seems to really care
If I come here at all
And the one who seems to care the least is you

I'm gonna hang a neon sign
With letters big and blue
Home Motel on Lost Love Avenue

I could have talked about this song in the *Abandoned Houses* chapter. It's all about a man who has lost his home and maybe his soul. His life is in shambles, his heart shattered in a million pieces.

I've waited to include it in this *Teatro* section, though, because just like they say that love can be lovelier the second time around, so can a song.

In the early sixties, when I was a young singer-songwriter hungry for a hit, I walked in the studio and saw a whole cadre of musicians playing a worked-up arrangement. I was impressed. And also confused. I didn't write "Home Motel" with violins and cellos in mind. I had nothing in mind except the character of a lost man in a lost world.

In Oxnard, California, during the *Teatro* sessions, the song was stripped down to its bones. I didn't even play Trigger. I didn't use Bobbie or Mickey or any of my regulars. It was just my voice and the piano of Brad Mehldau. It was stark. And dark.

Maybe that's why I was able to see the street with a laundromat, a liquor store, and a motel. The big blue neon light had burned out. Some of the windows were busted. But on the top floor a dim light bulb showed the face of a man who still lived there. He was old. He was bereft. But he still had a song to sing. It might have been the only song he had ever sung, the one song he had always been destined to sing.

Emmylou Harris, Daniel Lanois, and I take a break from recording *Teatro*.

I JUST CAN'T LET YOU SAY GOODBYE

I had not planned on seeing you
I was afraid of what I'd do
But pride is strong, and here am I
I just can't let you say goodbye

Please have no fear, you're in no harm
As long as you're here in my arms
But you can't leave so please don't try
But I just can't let you say goodbye

What force behind your evil mind
Can let your lips speak so unkind
To one who loves as much as I
But I just can't let you say goodbye

The flesh around your throat is pale
Indented by my fingernails
Please don't scream, please don't cry
'Cause I just can't let you say goodbye

Your voice is still, it speaks no more
You'll never hurt me anymore
Death is a friend to love and I
'Cause now you'll never say goodbye

Maybe it's more a movie than a song. Maybe it's a film noir. Maybe it's a moment when I let go of my traditional thinking about songwriting and did something different. Even dangerous. I felt that danger when I sang this song back in 1968 and felt it again twenty years later in the empty movie house.

On the screen a man waits in a car across from an art deco apartment building in old Hollywood. He waits for hours. The moon is a sliver in the sky. The streetlight is on the blink. The streets are deserted. He smokes one cigarette after another. He drains his flask of whiskey. He nearly nods out. But he's awake enough to see a woman leave the lobby of the building. She gets in her car and drives off.

Knowing a shortcut, he arrives at their home before she does. When she walks through the door, he's seated in his leather armchair, cracked and worn.

"Where you been?" he asks.

"Out with my girlfriends."

"Doing what?"

"We went to a movie."

"Which one?"

"*Double Indemnity*. What did you do tonight, honey?"

"Just sat here and wrote a song."

"Can I hear it?"

"Sure. Come over here and I'll sing it to you."

I'VE JUST DESTROYED THE WORLD

The sun just went behind the clouds
There's darkness all around me now
And I've just destroyed the world I'm living in

I broke her heart so many times
And now at last I've broken mine
And I've just destroyed the world I'm living in

What made me think that I could go on hurting her
I had to know there had to be an end

But fools in love are taught by faith
We never learn till it's too late
And I've just destroyed the world I'm living in

Even though this song sounds like the follow-up to the murderous "I Just Can't Let You Say Goodbye," it was actually written earlier. And I also didn't do it alone.

My faithful friend and mentor Ray Price wrote it with me when I was just getting going in Nashville. He recorded it in 1966 on his album *The Same Old Me*. I can't remember which lyrics or notes were written by me and which by Ray. All I can recall is talking about how men have a way of screwing up relationships with women.

I can still hear Ray saying, "You got that right, Willie. But maybe rather than talk about it, we'd do better to sing about it."

Next thing we knew, we had us a song.

"Destruction" is a heavy word, and *Teatro* is a heavy album. And even though you can see that destruction—destroying a love, destroying a man, even destroying the life of a woman—as a major theme, *Teatro* was also about reconstruction.

What Ray and I had written those many years earlier was renewed in a very different way in that drafty old movie house.

A deeply dark song was recast in a new light.

And although some might call it gloomy, I didn't see it that way. In talking about the end of the world, Ray and I had written a new beginning.

A song is constructed about destruction only to be reconstructed. And reconstruction, like all creative work, goes on forever.

"But maybe rather than talk about it, we'd do better to sing about it."

SOMEBODY PICK UP MY PIECES

Somebody pick up my pieces
I'm scattered everywhere
And put me back together
Put me way over there

Take me out of contention
I surrender my crown
Somebody pick up my pieces
It's just me coming down

Well, I sure thought I had her
Lord, I know she had me
But what I thought was heaven
Is just falling debris

Well, I may not be crazy
But I got one hell of a start
Somebody pick up my pieces
I think I'm falling apart

And don't follow my footsteps
Step over my trail
The road is too narrow
And your footing could fail

And the fall to the bottom
Could tear you apart
And they'll be picking up pieces
Of you and your heart

Critics never bother me, mainly because I don't read them. Never have, and have no plans to start.

I don't dislike critics—aside from your unavoidable asshole, I like most people—and I understand that, like a tax collector or a truant officer, critics have a job to do. Their job doesn't bother me. As long as folks come to my shows and have a good time, critics can criticize till they're blue in the face.

Occasionally, before I have time to object, a friend will read me something someone has written about my music. That's how I heard about a critic who said Willie Nelson uses misery in his songs because misery is romantic.

Now that's a helluva statement.

If I say in a song, "Somebody pick up my pieces because I'm falling apart and, for God's sake, don't follow my lead or you'll fall apart yourself," you could safely conclude misery is the message. But if there's a connection to romance, the connection is pretty loose. The romance is more than tarnished; it's ruined.

Is ruined romance the same as true romance?

You tell me.

THREE DAYS

Three days that I hate to see arrive
Three days that I hate to be alive
Three days filled with tears and sorrow
Yesterday, today, and tomorrow

There are three days that I know that
    I'll be blue
Three days that I'll always dream of you

But it does no good to wish these days
    would end
'Cause the same three days start over again

Three days that I hate to see arrive
Three days that I dread to be alive
Three days filled with tears and sorrow
Yesterday, today, and tomorrow

360

Unlike some of my learned associates, I've never read the poet T. S. Eliot. One of those associates pointed out that what I thought was a pretty simple song, one that boiled down to three words—"Three Days"—might have complex implications. Naturally, I asked for a fuller explanation. Had I written something even I didn't understand?

I was quoted these lines from Eliot:

"Time present and time past / Are both perhaps present in time future, / And time future contained in time past. / If all time is eternally present / All time is unredeemable."

Holy cow!

Is that what I was saying in my song?

Maybe. Maybe I was saying that this love is unredeemable. Maybe I was saying that this dying love will always live because it thrives outside of time. Maybe I was also saying that the past love, the present love, and the future love all get mixed up in mind. And my mind won't let that love go.

Or maybe I wasn't saying any of that.

Maybe I was just saying that this woman drives me nuts.

I'VE LOVED YOU
ALL OVER THE WORLD

You're my buddy, my pal, my friend
It will be that way until the end
And wherever you go, I want you to know
You're my buddy, my pal, my friend

And I've loved you all over the world
You are my sunshine
You keep my life in a whirl
And you love me sometimes

I'll always follow my heart
Wherever it takes me
And until death do us part
I'll love you all over the world

Think of all my
songs as gifts to you.

If "Three Days" may have invited a bunch of heady interpretations, the same can't be said for "I've Loved You All Over the World."

What you hear is what you get.

The only question might involve the title:

"Who is 'you'?"

The only answer is obvious:

"You is you."

I'm not trying to be a wise guy. I mean it.

Think of this song as a gift to you. Think of all my songs as gifts to you. In the old days, those gifts were free when you heard them on the radio. These days, with streaming services and digital downloads, they're even freer.

Well, I'm still free to sing to myself in the shower. I can sing to myself sitting on the back porch wondering whether the dark clouds mean rain. I can sing to myself riding on the bus from Cheyenne to Chicago. And sometimes I do. There's pleasure in solitary singing. But man, it's nothing compared to singing in front of live human beings when I'm connecting to your heart and you're connecting to mine.

That connection carries a warmth and love that's beyond the power of mere words. It's just something I feel. Something I cherish. Something I live for.

ANNIE

The final song on *Teatro* is an instrumental I wrote for my wife Annie.

I was going to put words to it, but Annie asked me not to.

When I asked her why, she said, "Our feelings for each other are precious, but private. And I'd like to keep it that way."

So I have.

CANNIBALISM
(or stealing from myself)

I've never wanted to be one of those writers who takes himself too seriously.

I liked it when my good buddy Leon Russell, in "A Song for You," wrote that he'd made some bad rhymes. Me too. I've also repeated myself. I don't consider that a mortal sin, since there's only so much I have to say.

Like comics, all songwriters borrow from one another. After all, there are only twelve notes. Sometimes that borrowing is unconscious and sometimes it's intentional.

It doesn't bother me that I've borrowed—hell, I've flat-out stolen from myself.

In the spirit of full disclosure, I'd like to point out a couple of instances of Willie ripping off Willie. I'm sure there are many more examples, but when it comes to self-indictment, a little goes a long way.

A FOOL IN THE FIRST DEGREE

Crossed the line, broke the rules
Cheated me, cheating you
Broke your soul, killed your smile
Missed the mark by a mile
I'm a fool in the first degree

Look it up and there I'll be
Perfect you, stupid me
I'm a fool in the first degree

I'm a fool, a four-letter word
But why tell you what you already heard
When you think "loser," you think of me
I'm a fool in the first degree

I don't go to funerals and I won't be at mine
I'll be in heaven or hell doing my time
If you want wrong, leave it to me
I'm a fool in the first degree

Don't blame my cowriter Buddy Cannon for the steal. He didn't swipe a line of lyrics from an old song. I did.

I set out to write a song of self-indictment. The indictment wasn't against the storyteller copying himself, but the storyteller admitting that he'd been a dog.

The character I created gets so caught up in that admission that he loses his train of thought. That train has him going straight to hell—heaven is just wishful thinking—and there is no going back. There aren't enough bad things he could say about himself.

But he does something I've had other characters do in other songs: In "Goin' Home" from *Yesterday's Wine*, my man witnesses his own funeral. Maybe, later in my life, that didn't seem like such a good idea. So I flipped the switch and named a song "I Don't Go to Funerals." I thought it would be clever to add, "And I won't be at mine."

If it was clever once, it could be clever twice. Maybe that's foolish thinking. But in a song that's all about being a fool, I thought the line fit.

Plus, it's the truth.

With Leon Russel, having some fun.

YOUR MEMORY HAS A MIND OF ITS OWN

Your memory has a mind of its own
It knows where to go when it's gone
I think I've lost it, then it proves me wrong
Your memory has a mind of its own

I can't tell it what to do
I can smoke and I can drink till it's out of view
But I can't hold it off, it's too strong
Your memory has a mind of its own

Your memory does what it wants to do
It survives though I don't want it to
I do okay when I don't think of you
But your memory does what it wants to do

If your memory had ears they'd be burning
If your memory had eyes they'd be crying
And if it had a heart it would leave me alone
But your memory has a mind of its own

My memory might have a mind of its own, but my memory might also be shot to hell. That's not a bad thing, because if my memory was super-sharp, I might have recalled having written "Love Has a Mind of Its Own" with Hank Cochran. And that might have stopped me from repeating the phrase when, a lifetime later, I wrote "Your Memory Has a Mind of Its Own" with Buddy Cannon. Over fifty years separate the two songs.

Lousy memory or not, I'm sticking to my guns when it comes to my beliefs.

I do believe love has a mind of its own.

And I do believe memory is going to go wherever it wants to go.

We don't control love and we don't control memory. We don't control much of anything. And the more we try to control, the more miserable we become. Frustration builds. Relaxation flies out the window. Creativity shuts down.

Creativity needs to flow.

Memory and love need to flow.

And it looks like some of my songs flow backward—picking up old ideas and placing them in new positions—and some flow forward, heading into directions I won't understand until I get there.

And it looks like some of my songs flow backward.

• EPILOGUE •

Energy Follows Thought

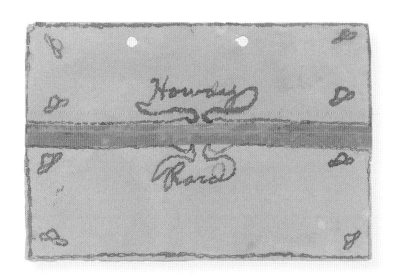

ENERGY FOLLOWS THOUGHT

Imagine what you want
Then get out of the way
Remember energy follows thought
So be careful what you say

Be careful what you ask for
Make sure it's really what you want
Because your mind is made for
   thinking
And energy follows thought

Your mind is in control
Even when you do not know
And if you let it idle
Ain't no telling where it'll go

Wherever you are sleeping
And your dreams take you away
Go on with your dreaming
And listen to what they say

And if you hear spirits talking
Their wisdom can't be bought
Apply it to your thinking
And energy follows thought

Your mind is in control
Even when you do not know
And if you let it idle
Ain't no telling where it'll go

My friends are always saying kind things to me, especially the musicians in my band.

Mickey Raphael, who knows my songs as well as anyone, recently told me that "Energy Follows Thought" is probably the best one I've ever written. Quite a compliment, since I wrote the thing, along with Buddy Cannon, when I was deep in my eighties. Thanks, Mickey, but I'm not inclined to rank my songs any more than a mother is inclined to rank her children.

The idea behind "Energy Follows Thought" is something I've been saying for a long time. It just took me eight decades to be able to say it in a simple way that makes sense.

I guess you could call it a summing-up.

As I sum up, I feel that it's time for me to stop writing about my songs and start writing a new one.

Time to start writing *Energy Follows Thought: Volume 2* . . .

• ACKNOWLEDGMENTS •

David Ritz would like to thank Willie for being Willie; Mickey Raphael for his insights and knowledge; Mark Rothbaum for his many creative ideas; David Vigliano for having our back; Mauro DiPreta for great editing; and Mauro's superb team: Martha Cipolla, copyeditor; Bonni Leon-Berman, book designer; Brian Moore, jacket designer; Amanda Hong, production editor; and Allie Johnston, editorial assistant. Love to my wife Roberta, family & friends who keep me going strong.

Mickey Raphael would like to thank Willie Nelson for fifty years of therapy through his amazing lyrics, David Ritz for his amazing writing, his invaluable insight, and agreeing to all my song choices, Mark Rothbaum for the opportunities and creative guidance, Mauro DiPreta, David Vigliano, and Rob Finan for making things happen, and Adrienne Gerard and Allison Brandin for wrangling every photo ever taken of Willie.

• CREDITS •

SONG LYRICS

PHOTOGRAPHS

frontispiece: © Scott Newton

Page 3: © Mark Seliger/AUGUST Image, LLC

Page 5: Courtesy of The Wittliff Collections, Texas State University

Page 8: All photos courtesy of The Wittliff Collections, Texas State University

Page 9: All photos courtesy of The Wittliff Collections, Texas State University

Page 10: © The Estate of David Gahr via Getty Images

Page 12: Michael Ochs Archives via Getty Archives

Page 14: © Scott Newton

Page 16: © Scott Newton

Page 18: © Photojournalist Jimmy Moore

Page 20: Dave G. Houser via Getty Images

Page 21: © 1973 JD Sloan

Page 23: © Henry Horenstein/AUGUST Image, LLC

Page 24: The Estate of David Gahr via Getty Images

Page 26: © Lana Nelson

Page 29: Courtesy of the Country Music Hall of Fame® and Museum

Page 30: © Scott Newton

Page 32: © Jimmy Ellis – USA TODAY NETWORK

Page 39: Neil Leifer via Getty Images

Page 40: Fair use

Page 44: Bettmann via Getty Images

Page 46: From the collection of Mickey Raphael

Page 50: © 1982 Alan Messer

Page 52: © Jan Sikes

Page 58: © Scott Newton

Page 60: Courtesy of Sony Music Entertainment / Photograph by Photojournalist Jimmy Moore

Page 64: Courtesy of Sony Music Entertainment / Photograph by Photojournalist Jimmy Moore

Page 66: © Chris Cuffaro/AUGUST Image, LLC

Page 73: © Lana Nelson

Page 75: © Lana Nelson

Page 78: © Jim Steinfeldt/Cache Agency

Page 86: © 1975 Robert W. Hart

Page 90: © Scott Newton

Page 92: © George V. Fowler

Page 94: © Lana Nelson

Page 97: © Everett Collection Historical / Alamy Stock Photo

Page 98: © Scott Newton

Page 101: © Melinda Wickman Swearingen

Page 105: © Burton Wilson

Page 109: © 1972 Jim Marshall Photography LLC

Page 110: Richard E. Aaron via Getty Images

Page 113: © Scott Newton

Page 114: © M Andrews Photography

Page 118: Licensed by Thomas Sims Archives/Reelin' In The Years Productions LLC

Page 120: © Ron McKeown

Page 125: © Ebet Roberts/Cache Agency

Page 130: Courtesy of Universal Music Enterprises

Page 132: Courtesy of The Wittliff Collections, Texas State University

Page 134: © Danny Garrett

Page 136: © Scott Newton

Page 138: Steve Brooks Collection, University of North Texas Special Collections

Page 140: Fair use

Page 143: © Scott Newton

Page 144: From the collection of Mickey Raphael

Page 145 (left): © Buddy Prewitt

Page 145 (right): Fair use

Page 149: © Burton Wilson

Page 150: © Rick Henson Photography

Page 152: Courtesy of The Wittliff Collections, Texas State University

Page 154: Fair use

Page 156: © Lana Nelson

Page 158: Courtesy of Sony Music Entertainment / Photograph by Photojournalist Jimmy Moore

Page 159: Fort Worth Star-Telegram via Getty Images

Page 160: From the collection of Mickey Raphael

Page 163: The Estate of David Gahr via Getty Images

Page 164: © Lana Nelson

Page 167: © Rick Henson Photography

Page 173: © Michael Abramson

· INDEX ·

Page numbers in *italics* refer to photographs or their captions.

I see
these lyrics
as little
postcards
from a
long life.

· THE AUTHORS ·

Willie Nelson has won a dozen Grammys, the Library of Congress Gershwin Prize, and the Kennedy Center Honors. For more than seven decades, his records have topped the charts the world over. He has written bestselling books, starred in films, and supported environmental and Native American causes as well as the legalization of cannabis. He is a cofounder of Farm Aid.

David Ritz, the author of sixty books, has collaborated with everyone from Aretha Franklin to Ray Charles. He cowrote "Sexual Healing" with Marvin Gaye.

Mickey Raphael, one of the country's leading harmonica players, has been a member of Willie's Family band for fifty years. He's performed on hundreds of albums and has served as a producer and arranger.

HarperCollins books may be purchased for educational, business, or sales promotional use. For information, please email the Special Markets Department at SPsales@harpercollins.com.

FIRST EDITION

Designed by Bonni Leon-Berman

Library of Congress Cataloging-in-Publication Data has been applied for.

ISBN 978-0-06-327220-0

23 24 25 26 27 TC 10 9 8 7 6 5 4 3 2 1

this is the very first day since y

that I've tried to put my thoughts

and all I can hear myself say

is I still can't believe your gone

I still can't believe your gone

What did I do that was so wrong

there are too many questions unan

and I still can't believe your go

But your gone and I'm still here so

sorry—

I don't like it but I'd take it up

But oh it's been so long now co

and I still can't believe your gon